HANDBOOK OF ANCIENT GREEK AND ROMAN COINS

by Zander H. Klawans
Edited by K. E. Bressett

WHITMAN® COIN PRODUCTS

Copyright ©1995 by
Western Publishing Company, Inc.
Racine, Wisconsin 53404
All Rights Reserved

9362   ISBN 0-307-09362-X   Printed in U.S.A.

INTRODUCTION

This is not a new book. It is a combination of two primary references that have been used by collectors for over 30 years. Both were originally authored by Zander H. Klawans, and were published in several modified editions. Both have suffered from the need of revision brought about by modern research and newly discovered data.

In his first book, *Reading and Dating Roman Imperial Coins,* Zander Klawans attempted to write a handbook for beginners that would provide a clear understanding of the subject by exposing collectors to all aspects of the coins. It was not intended to replace any of the classic texts, but rather to provide useful answers to frequently asked questions.

His second book covered the older coins of another culture and was entitled *An Outline of Ancient Greek Coins.* This too was not a story book, but rather a useful tool for learning about the myriad aspects of ancient coins and what they meant to the people who used them. It is replete with facts and information necessary to understand these fascinating coins, as well as incorporating hundreds of photographs to show exactly what is being discussed.

Even the casual reader of ancient history knows that Athens, during the fifth century B.C., was the shrine of knowledge, the most remarkable arena in all history, past or present, for the demonstration of human capabilities. Both Greek and Roman coins are a part of that enrichment, and this book illustrates how money, art and history all blend together.

Ancient coins have advanced considerably in price in the years since Klawans' books were first published, but it is still possible to purchase specimens at prices that surely must be considered bargains. Yet, regardless of price, how can we place a value on the experience of holding in our hand a little fragment of the past? The tremendous growth of interest in collecting these coins over the years is largely due to the availability of handy references like the Klawan's books which make the subject easy to grasp.

It was my great pleasure to know Zander Klawans, to share his warm friendship for many years, and to have the opportunity to assist with publication of his original books. It is now the hope of this editor that combining the works of Klawans into one handy volume will aid both beginners and advanced students. There is probably nothing in this book that can not be found in other references, but here it is laid out in a manner that is assessable and easy to follow. If it serves that purpose it will meet our original hope of fostering new interest in this delightful adventure.

Ken Bressett
September 1994

PART I

AN OUTLINE OF
ANCIENT
GREEK COINS

by

Zander H. Klawans

Greek Italy

Greece and Asia Minor

THRACIA

MARONEA

THASUS

AENUS

ISTRUS

PERINTHUS

BYZANTIUM

CALCHEDON

BITHYNIA

CYZICUS

LAMPSACUS

ABYDOS

IMBROS

MYSIA

LEMNOS

TENEDOS

METHYMNA

LESBOS

MITILENE

PERGAMUM

PHRYGIA

SARDES

CHIOS

ERYTH

CLAZOMENAE

SMYRNA

LYDIA

TEOS

LEBEDOS

EPHESUS

MAGNESIA AD MAEANDRUM

IKARIA

SAMOS

TRALLES

MILET

NAXOS

CARIA

KALYMNA

KOS

CNIDUS

ANAPHE

LINDUS

RHODUS

ELEUTHERNA

CNOSSUS

ITANUS

LYTTUS

PHAESIUS

GORTYNA

HIERAPYTNA

THE BIRTH OF A COIN

The manufacture of ancient Greek coins becomes all the more remarkable when we ponder the means by which they were made. In this mass-producing age of ours it is difficult to imagine that these early coins were individually created under conditions far from ideal.

First it was necessary for the artist, or his assistants, to make dies. This he did by carving (intaglio) into a thick bronze disk which fitted into an anvil (illustration No. 1B, inset). This was the obverse, or lower die. Then, at the base of a punch (No. 1E, inset), he would carve the reverse die.

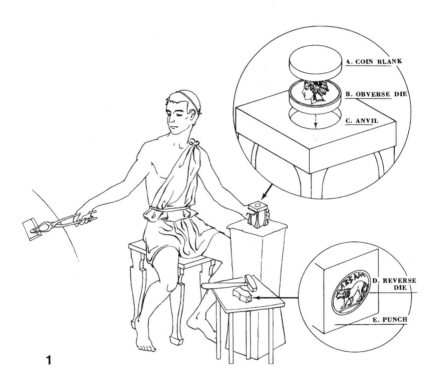

1

Finished dies were used to strike blanks of metal that were either heated or, more often, cold. If heated the workman, using tongs, would reach into the furnace and grasp the metal blank which had been kept at the correct temperature and place it upon the obverse die seated in the anvil (No. 2, page 12). He would then take his hammer and the punch containing the reverse die and place the punch upon the blank in the anvil. A sharp blow with his hammer, or often more than one blow, and a coin had been made (No. 3, page 12). It was now necessary only to remove the coin from the anvil and allow it to cool.

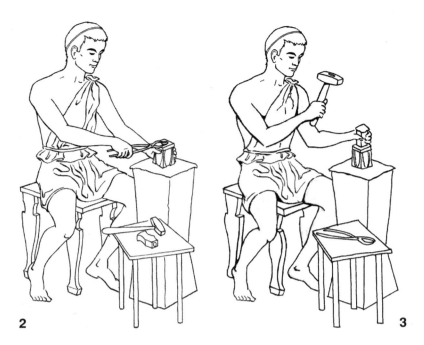

2   **3**

Understanding this process one may realize, also, why we find so many coins struck weakly or off center or even double struck. Few such workmen were concerned with creating works of art or had an eye for

Coin of Arverni. First century B.C.

posterity. Their job was to make coins and they did so with varying talents. Under such circumstances it is remarkable that so many fine specimens have come down to us.

It is well to know that the method discussed here did not apply to the manufacture of all coins. The earliest Greek coins had only an obverse

Coin of Aeneia. Fifth century B.C.

image and the reverse simply showed sharp punch marks from a punch which had been designed to exert pressure upon the coin.

AN INTRODUCTION TO GREEK COINAGE

Throughout the ages the art of coinage, as would be true of any art, has attracted both craftsmen and the untalented. Many of the works of these diverse personalities remain with us to this day. Some of these coins are, indeed, a joy to behold. Others are very crude. Yet, more important than any consideration from an artistic standpoint is the fact that these small tokens spread before us a segment of man's highest achievement, the story of what he can do, if he has a mind to do it. It would seem that one would possess an insensitive and untutored heart not to feel himself swept into some form of communion with brothers who long ago fell

into the arms of their gods. Surely, there is little beauty in one of the first coinages known to man, this electrum piece struck in ancient Lydia (or Ionia, both in what is now western Turkey), yet the significance of this coinage is overwhelming. This was the idea, in fact, of such force and magnitude as to escape the imagination of its creator. We could say, and without contradiction, that this was the beginning of our own coinage.

It is indeed difficult to look at this coin of Darius the Great of Persia without finding our minds rushing back to that soft plain edging into the sea at Marathon, seeing there the heroic Greeks beating the superior Persian forces back into the sea while one of their numbers, Pheidippides, runs to Sparta, there to plead hopelessly for aid. Had the Athenians lost, would Europe have been as we know it today?

To this day we speak of someone being "rich as Croesus," 2500 years after the death of that king. Coins struck during his time display the symbols of power, a bull and a lion facing one another.

The tiny island of Aegina in the Saronikon Gulf, not too far from Athens, has the distinction of being the first community in Greece proper to strike coins. Upon these coins we see the turtle, one of the famous symbols of Greek money.

The Macedonian Greeks, a rustic and virile lot, placed figures of satyrs and nymphs upon their coinage engaged in a lusty pursuit of bodily pleasures. In this rugged section of the Greek mainland there were few inhibitions.

As time moved on, other cities struck coins and affixed a distinctive symbol upon them. The city of Corinth on the Corinthian Gulf placed Pegasos, the flying horse, upon her coins. The word "pegasos" means "strong" in Greek and the symbol was an accurate one for Corinth at one time possessed great power.

Sybaris, in southern Italy, lost a war to her neighbors of Kroton who diverted a river over the desolated city, inundating it and probably losing it forever. We have derived a word from the name of this town; we call one who lives luxuriously a sybarite. As an item of interest, note that the reverse of the coin is incuse with a design that mirrors the obverse.

The Krotonians mentioned above used a tripod upon their coins.

Metapontum, also in Italy, placed an ear of corn upon her coins possibly in homage to Demeter, goddess of the grain.

Upon the coinage of Taras, or Tarentum (present day Taranto) we find a boy riding a dolphin. This symbol was derived from an ancient myth which told of Taras who was saved from a shipwreck by a dolphin which had been sent by his father, the god Poseidon. The dolphin swam to shore and at the point of landing the city was established.

Athens had always been known for the little owls which appeared upon her coinage. These wide-eyed birds were known throughout the Greek world.

Thus, city after city began to strike coinage. Through the use of coinage, trade increased, competition grew. It must be remembered that there was little unity among the cities of Greece at any time. Each city was power unto itself and it was only upon occasion that the cities banded together in a confederation.

GREEK COIN DENOMINATIONS

It is of interest to know the various denominations of Greek coins so that they may properly be identified. It should be remembered, however, that while many of the coins possess a common name, they may have varied in weight throughout the Greek world. As an example, the DRACHM varied in weight from 56 grains under the standard of the Phoenicians to 97 grains under the Aegenetic standard. The term stater, as another example, was synonymous with drachm, at times, or the didrachm, or even the tetradrachm.

The largest coin, and one not too frequently seen, was the DEKADRACHM (pronounced DEKADRAM). The Syracusans of Greek Sicily created some magnificent, perhaps the most magnificent, coins in this denomination. (DEKA means ten in Greek, thus ten times the drachm.)

The TETRADRACHM (Tetra, meaning four. Thus four times the drachm).

The DIDRACHM (pronounced DYDRAM. DI, meaning two. Two times the drachm).

The DRACHM

The OBOL

The DIOBOL
(Twice the obol).

The TRIOBOL (Three times the obol
and one half the drachm. Six obol,
then, would be the equivalent of one
drachm).

The TETROBOL (Four times the obol).

The TRIHEMIOBOL (Three times one
half an obol).

The HEMIOBOL (one half obol).

The beginning collector probably will not spend too much time with the gold coins of ancient Greece because of their cost and because of their rarity. However, some of the principal coins are mentioned as an item of interest.

There were many different types of coins issued. Some were fractional subdivisions of larger coins, particularly the gold stater. From Kyrene in Kyrenacia, now Libya, in Africa, come a number of these coins. Some are pictured below.

The Gold Stater

1/4 Gold Stater

1/10 Gold Stater

And from Carthage, the great Semitic stronghold in Africa, comes the electrum stater, a coin made of gold and silver.

The Ptolemies, inheritors of Alexander the Great's Egyptian empire, struck some beautiful gold coins. Among them we find:

Gold Octodrachm of Arsinoe, wife of Ptolemy II

Gold Tetradrachm of Ptolemy I

Gold Pentadrachm of Ptolemy II

From Persia we have the famous coin of Darius II, called the DARIC.

Darius the III of Persia struck a gold coin called a DOUBLE DARIC.

From the island called Lesbos in ancient days (now Mytilene), home of the great poetess Sappho, comes a gold and silver coin called an ELECTRUM HEKTON.

Stater of electrum (natural mixture of silver and gold)

1/6 Electrum Stater   *1/12 Electrum Stater*   *1/24 Electrum Stater*

Kyzicus in ancient Mysia (now northwestern Turkey) struck a number of electrum coins also, the sizes of which must have made them particularly difficult to handle. Note that these coins are fractional portions of the larger electrum stater.

Imagine carrying a number of these last coins about in your pocket! After all, they were gold coins in part so the loss of them could not be treated lightly.

The reader should remember that all of the coins have not been mentioned. Some are of too great a rarity; others were limited to and peculiar to certain communities, as are some of those illustrated.

HOW TO READ THE COINS

It is not the proper purpose of this book to take up the subject of Greek pronunciation or Greek grammar. It is sufficient to say that much of the Greek taught in this country is in an "Anglicized" or "Americanized" version. As an example, we think of the letter "G," the Greek gamma, as sounding exactly as it reads. However, in certain instances it adopts a nasal quality so that we have a "g" which sounds like the "ng" in SING. The result is a gamma which would sound more like YAMMA. This nasal, or gamma nasal as it is called, occurs before Kappa, Xi or Chi. The god Zeus who appears upon so many of the coins more properly would be called ZEFFS, because the diphthong "eu" has the sound of "eff." Many of the other diphthongs in Greek are similar to our own and so we find that "ai" is sounded as in "aisle," "ei" as in "eight," "oi" as in

19

"oil," "au" as in "our," "ui" as in "quit," and "ou" as in "group." It is also well for the reader to remember that there is no equivalent for our letter H in Greek. There is a letter which looks like our H, but it is the E, or Eta. The reason many words in Greek sound as if they begin with H is due to the fact that some are spoken with what might be called "rough breathing," others with "smooth breathing." Thus, the very word for Greek which would look like Hellenikos, from Hellene, actually has no letter "H" to start and is spelled, in Greek, ELLENIKOS. This is an example of "rough breathing" and the sound is aspirated. If the reader will say the word to himself a few times, exhaling though his mouth, he shall see that the letter "H" is formed automatically. An example of "smooth breathing" or an unaspirated word would be the name of the Greek goddess, Artemis. Obviously, it would be incorrect to call her HARTEMIS.

In learning to read the coins of Greece it is necessary, at first, to refer to the Greek alphabet. For the sake of clarity the alphabet has been divided into four columns. The first column carries numerals before the letters. These numerals indicate the numerical equivalents of the letters which are opposite them. The numerals are shown because they appear upon certain coins of Greek Egypt and are used as a means of dating these coins. Before the reader evinces enthusiasm over this statement it must be mentioned that such dating is not arrived at by any means which would be common to our civilization, with one exception. Such dating was calculated from some specific incident or the reign of a specific king. Thus, it is necessary for us to know that incident or reign in order to arrive at the date of the coin. The one example in usage today would be the dating of our own American coins from the time of Christ. Briefly, the word "probably" is one used with great frequency by Greek scholars in such dating. Barclay Head, who devoted his life to the subject, says, in the revised edition of his HISTORIA NUMORUM, that the Ptolemies of Egypt usually dated their money by the regnal years of the king, though some series appear to be dated from the era of Soter, 311B.C.; that others probably are dated from the deification of Arsinoe in 270 B.C. The number of possibilities and probabilities would extend beyond the field of this book, but the numerals are included as a matter of interest.

The second column contains the Greek letter itself. Inasmuch as the Greeks had no mechanical means of stamping their coins, as we understand mechanics, it must always be carried in the mind that the letters upon the coins, for the most part, are irregular and, in some instances, can be quite crude.

The third column spells out the letter.

The last two columns sound out the word phonetically.

Number	Letter	Name	Modern American Pronunciation	Modern Greek Pronunciation
1	A	ALPHA	Alfa	Alfa
2	B	BETA	Bayta	Veeta
3	Γ	GAMMA	Gamma	Yamma
4	Δ	DELTA	Delta	Thelta
5	ϵ E	EPSILON	Epsilon	Epsilon
7	Z I	ZETA	Zayta	Zeeta
8	H	ETA	Ayta	Eeta
9	⊖ ⊙	THETA	Thayta	Theeta
10	I	IOTA	Eye Ota	Eeota
20	K Q (KOPPA)	KAPPA	Kappa	Kappa
30	Λ ⌁	LAMBDA	Lambda	Lamtha
40	M	MU	Mew	Moo
50	N	NU	New (as in you)	Noo
60	≡ Ξ	XI	Zeye (as in eye)	Ksee
70	O	OMICRON	Omicron	Omicron
80	Π Π Γ	PI	Pye	Pee
100	P R (Rare)	RHO	Rowe (as in know)	Rowe (as in know)
200	Σ C Ϛ	SIGMA	Sigma	Siyamma
300	T	TAU	Tau (as in chaw)	Toff
400	Y V	UPSILON	Youpsilon	Ipsilon
500	φ	PHI	Phy	Phee
600	X	CHI	Keye (as in eye)	Chee
700	ψ	PSI	Sigh	Psee
800	Ω ω	OMEGA	Omayga	Omayga

Again mentioning the numerical equivalents in column one, the date is arrived at by adding the letters together. Thus, GDE (Gamma-Delta-Epsilon) would be 3 plus 4 plus 5, or 12. HKT (Eta-Kappa-Tau) would be 8 plus 20 plus 300, or 328.

Examining the alphabet, it must be an unmistakable observation that it is much similar to our own and, after all, we are indebted to the Greeks, and before them, to the Phoenicians, for at least a part of our alphabet. Even the word "alphabet" is a combined form of Alpha-Beta, the first two words of the Greek alphabet, from the Semitic words Aleph-Beth. It will also be noticed that the sounds of the letters are quite similar to our own. Using this table should be of great help in deciphering the coins.

For example, let us take one of the common words appearing upon the coins, the word for king, which is ΒΑΣΙΛΕΟΣ. The coin sounds as it reads BASILAYOS. Illustrated are coins of King Demetrios and King Antigonos. Both were kings of Macedonia, Demetrios ruling from 306-283 B.C. and Antigonos from 277-239 B.C. In examining the coin of Demetrios above, we find the word for king, ΒΑΣΙΛΕΟΣ, behind the standing figure of the god Poseidon. In front of the god appears the name of the king ΔΗΜΕΤΡΙΟΥ. Spelling it out, we have DELTA, ETA, MU, EPSILON, TAU, RHO (the Rho, "P," is not our letter "P," but an "R"), IOTA, OMICRON, UPSILON. Combine these letters and we have Demetriou…Demetrios. This ending, incidentally, that is, the ending OU is the genitive (possessive) singular ending in Greek. The word for king appearing upon this coin and ending in ΟΣ also is in the genitive case. Thus, the coin would read, "Of Demetrios the King," meaning that the coin was struck by him…was one of his coins.

Similarly, the coin of Antigonos should provide little difficulty if we use the alphabet to decipher it. Here again, the word for king is in the genitive case and his name also is in the genitive case; thus, "Of Antigonos the King."

Many of the titles and names upon the coins are abbreviated, yet even in their abbreviated forms the reader should not have too much difficulty in deciphering them. For example, here is a coin of ancient Metapontum, a Greek city in Italy. Note that only the first part of the word appears upon the coin, META. If this is not enough to identify the coin, and it is, then the ear of corn, long identified as a symbol of Metapontum, should provide conclusive identification.

The Krotonians, also a Greeek people in lower Italy, struck coins with their name foreshortened upon them. Here is such a coin with a tripod upon it, a constantly recurring symbol for this community. The first letter we see is a strange one. It is known as a KOPPA, derived from an old semitic form. Thus, we see the abbreviated form of Kroton (actually there was no hard letter "C" in the Greek alphabet and while they are interchanged today...Croton...Kroton...the correct usage would be the letter "K" in all instances) ϘRO.

This is a coin of Bruttium struck by people of Greek origin living in Italy. Here, the entire name is spelled out and we see BPETTIΩN, Brettion in those days, called Bruttium by us. Note the ending (ΩN). Here is the genitive or possessive case, plural. And so we read, "Of the Bretii," or more elaborately, "Of the people of Bruttium."

A crab appears on the coin of Agrigentum (also known as Akragas) a famous Sicilian city. The name is abbreviated, AKPA, but these letters should provide sufficient information to identify the coin.

One of the most common symbols of all Greece was the little owl of Athens. At one time this symbol was known and respected throughout the known world. On this coin we see the little owl with the abbreviation **AΘE** appearing next to it. **AΘE**, of course, represents the first three letters of the word Athens.

From the Greek island of Crete in the Mediterranean, comes a coin based upon the famous fable of the Minotaur and the labyrinth and, upon it, we see the labyrinth or maze. Beneath the labyrinth we find the name of the Cretan city where it was struck, the most famous city in all Crete and, at one time, the largest city in Europe. The name of the city was Knossus. The genitive ending in the plural indicates that it was manufactured by the Knossians; thus, "Of the Knossians."

The home of Alexander the First was in Macedonia, the northern section of ancient Greece. The coin pictured shows the goddess Artemis and on the reverse, the words **ΜΑΚΕΔΟΝΩΝ ΠΡΩΤΗΣ**. **ΜΑΚΕΔΟΝΩΝ** means "Of the Macedonians." **ΠΡΩΤΗΣ** is the Greek word for "first."

It is necessary only to mention two other occurrences upon some of the coins. In early times, the letter "C" was used as the Sigma or "S." The other is the oddity of seeing some of the inscriptions appearing backwards upon the coins. These are known as retrograde inscriptions. Pictured are two coins of Hyria, a Greek city in Italy, also known as Ydina. One coin has the inscription in its normal way, the other, retrograde.

Certain coins may cause the student considerable confusion unless he recalls the endings of the titles. Illustrated is a coin of Acanthus in Macedonia. Note how the inscription reads around the coin. Where do we start reading the coin? Close examination will reveal an ON as part of the inscription, on the left side of the coin. This is a common ending and we must immediately realize that the A, or Alpha, at the top left-hand side of the coin is the beginning. Thus, we read **AKANΘION**.

And upon a coin of the Chalcidian League we see an ΩN ending which, we recall, is the possessive or genitive plural ending. Knowing this, we realize that we start with the X at the top of the coin and read around from there. Some of the letters have been worn by the ages; the starting X is almost illegible. The Δ is upside down to the eye, yet we read **XAΛKIΔEΩN**.

As a final example, here is a coin of Opontus in Locris on the southern part of the Greek mainland. This time, the ΩN is at the right side of the coin. If, therefore, this is the genitive ending, then the inscription begins on the left. Thus, we read **OΓONTIΩN**.

DATING THE COINS

The collector of Roman coins, particularly those coins of the early Empire can, given certain charts, readily dates his coins. Collectors of

Greek coins, unfortunately, are not so lucky. Here, the only "charts" are catalogs, reference books and the coins themselves whereby the collector can attempt to "match up" his own coins. An elaborate task! But this should not be disappointing because many things can be learned about a coin if one will have the patience to learn some of the common symbols and city names which appear upon them. It has been explained earlier that many communities had symbols which came to be recognized throughout the Greek world or, certainly, throughout a large area of the Greek world. There is the little owl which appears upon the Athenian coinage. Boeotian communities displayed a shield upon their coins; Aegina, a turtle; Metapontum, an ear of corn; Knossus, a labyrinth, and so on. True, such knowledge does not date a coin, but it will help, at least, to learn where it came from.

The texture and style of a coin is of utmost importance, at least in broadly dating a coin. At the risk of indulging in generalities, it will be seen that the earliest Greek coins were crudely made and had either punch marks on their reverses or a copy of the obverse, intaglio. (An example of such a coin will be found on pg. 119, Sybaris.) Only in later Greek coinage do we find both obverse and reverse appearing in the form we are used to seeing.

Examples of the broad classification periods described appear following:

THE PERIOD OF ARCHAIC ART
(680-480 B.C.)

In thinking of the coinage of this period which covers some 200 years, the word "archaic" in many instances aptly describes the coinage. Not only was this coinage crudely manufactured, but the execution of the engraving (the art work) also was crude. In examining these coins we must not allow ourselves to be too critical of what we see. We must remember that man was embarking upon a new adventure in a field completely foreign to him. His ideas would come slowly and painfully and, as in any other art, time alone would bring him to perfection.

The earliest coins often show a lack of refinement. Dimension had not as yet been learned. Knowledge of anatomy, perhaps at a high state in other fields, had not yet found itself upon the coinage. Perspective was almost unknown. Above all, art in itself probably was not considered to be of prime importance; the making of the money, however, was. Thus, one of the oldest coins known to man, a very rare coin, indeed, was this coin struck in Ionia or Lydia (now western Turkey) about 650 B.C. A single glance will indicate that is is but a pellet with scratch marks on one side and punch marks upon the other.

Another early coin was this one struck during the time of the Lydian king Croesus about 550 years before the time of Christ. Croesus was a man of great wealth and the figures upon the coin, a lion and a bull facing each other, were indications of strength.

And again from Ionia, comes a coin struck in the late 6th century B.C. showing a flying boar on the obverse and the familiar punch marks on the reverse. These punch marks, incidentally, are made when the hammer comes down upon the punch which thrusts the coin upon the die in the anvil.

From Aegina, an island lying in the Saronikon Gulf southwest of Athens, come the first coins struck in Greece proper. Prior to this time all coinage had been struck by cities in Asia Minor. Stamped upon this coin is the famous turtle, "trade-mark" of Aegina. This coin was struck sometime around 500 B.C.

This coin of Athens, struck between 500 and 485 B.C., and among the first coins to have figures upon both obverse and reverse, shows an improvement over earlier coinage, a beginning awareness of form such as we would know it today. True, the head of the goddess leaves something to be desired, as does the little owl, but there is something charming about this design.

The Macedonians, a rugged, bawdy and, apparently, a perfectly candid people, depicted nymphs and satyrs in various love scenes upon their coinage. This coin was struck between 500 and 480 B.C.

THE PERIOD OF TRANSITIONAL ART
(480-415 B.C.)

Something inside all men demands that they learn and grow and that they be given the freedom to develop to the extent of which they are capable. A manifestation of this development is no less discernible in the creation of art work upon the coinage than it is in any other art or science. Thus, during the so-called transitional period, the people who fashioned the coins slowly began to creep from the jungles of a primitive art into a world of deeper perception and of a more than casual understanding of the human form and of design as well. Here and there, one finds the touch, during this period of a fine hand, of remarkable talents of observation, even of a certain delicacy, much of which had been lacking.

Pictured, here, is a coin of the first Alexander of Macedon. Upon it is evidence of development, the form of the horse, the attention to muscular structure and the idea of motion. This coin was struck between 498 and 454 B.C., probably closer to 454, from its style. It is during this period

that the artisans of Syracuse began the work which, ultimately, would place them as the masters of all Greek coinage. As a matter of conjecture, it might have been some of these craftsmen who were the teachers of the great masters, artists such as Kimon, Euainetos, Herakleidas, Eukleidas and the one known only as the Aetna Master. In this coin there is a rhythm, a poetry of motion. The dolphins swimming about the head of Arethusa represent a fertility of imagination. The reverse, no less, displays a magnificent attention to detail; one could almost expect the horses to rush from the coin! This coin was struck between 466 and 425 B.C.

Selinos in Sicily possessed its share of artistic talent as this coin will testify. Here there is a freedom of motion about the entire piece and, upon the obverse, even violent motion, for Herakles, Hercules as we know him, has seized a bull by the horn and is about to slay him. The reverse figure, the river god Hypsas, is sacrificing at an altar. Note the muscular detail of the body. This coin was struck between 480 and 466 B.C.

The close of this period brought forward a magnificent coin of Agrigentum, in Sicily. Here, two eagles stand upon a captured hare, the one looking downward as if contemplating his catch, the other shrieking to the sky above him. This coin was struck between 413 and 406 B.C.

As the above coin indicates, it is now but a small step into the highest period of Greek art. We can almost say that the first two acts are finished, that the greatest performers now make their entrance upon the stage to present to us some of the most beautiful creations in all numismatics.

THE PERIOD OF FINEST ART
(415-336 B.C.)

For almost eighty years some of the loveliest and most inspired creations reached a height of magnificent perfection. In many instances the hands

of geniuses turned to the bronze dies expressing an almost unfathomable understanding of form. At Amphipolis in Macedonia (northern Greece) there was struck a coin, among others, with the head of Apollo upon it. Words would be inexpressive in describing such a coin; one need only glance at this masterpiece to realize the mastery of the artist who created it. This coin was struck between 424 and 358 B.C.

And from Syracuse in Sicily, where so many of the great masters worked, we see this coin from the hand of the great engraver, Kimon, displaying the head of Arethusa upon its reverse and a quadriga pulled by charging horses upon the obverse. This coin probably was struck around 408 B.C.

A similar coin, created by the master Euainetos, probably was struck about 390 B.C. Persephone graces the obverse.

Between the years 431 and 331 B.C. this beautiful gold stater was struck at Kyrene (now Libya, in Africa) demonstrating the high knowledge of anatomy on the part of the artist who created it.

A craftsman of Terina, in Italy, created this delicate coin picturing a nymph and, upon the reverse, the Nike, or winged victory. Time has erased some of the detail of the reverse, but the gracefulness of the figure remains. This coin might rightfully belong in the preceding period of transitional art yet, artistically, it seems to be more a part of this period of highest art.

Some unknown master at Kroton, in Italy, created this coin with the head of the goddess Hera upon it. There is something inescapably haunting about the face and one is almost reminded of the Mona Lisa. Is Hera smiling? This coin was struck sometime between 420 and 390 B.C.

THE PERIOD OF LATER FINE ART
(336-280 B.C.)

For the most part this period continues along the same high artistic level as the one preceding it. Particular notice should be given to the development of the head, brought to perfection. Muscular detail is brought forward in a startlingly realistic manner. We also find that many of the reverse figures are seated. A particularly famous coin of this period is the one of Alexander the Great which appears and reappears over a great period of time, having been struck not only during the time of Alexander, but also by his successors. The seated figure is that of the great god, Zeus. The obverse is that of Alexander as represented by Herakles (Hercules). This coin was struck between 336 and 323 B.C.

The famous Demetrius Poliorcetes who ruled Macedonia from 306 to 283 B.C. is pictured upon this beautiful tetradrachm struck during his rule. On the reverse we see Poseidon, god of the sea.

The Locrians, in Italy, introduced this didrachm with the image of Zeus upon the obverse and an eagle upon the reverse. The coin was struck sometime between 332 and 326 B.C.

Again, from Syracuse, this tetradrachm was struck during the time of the tyrant Agathocles (310-306 B.C.) Persephone graces the front of the coin and the Nike, or winged victory, the reverse.

Lysimachus, king of Thrace, and one of Alexander the Great's generals, saw this tetradrachm struck during his time (323-281 B.C.) Upon it is the deified head of Alexander and the goddess Pallas.

THE PERIOD OF THE DECLINE OF THE ART
(280-146 B.C.)

The word "decline" does not always apply to the coins struck during this period for many beautiful coins were struck. As a generality, the coinage of Asiatic Greece seems to have been created on a much higher level than that of European Greece.

The above coin may lack some of the high standards we have already seen in the periods of highest art, yet few would deny its beauty. It is a coin of Antiochus IV of Syria, a tetradrachm struck between 175 and 164 B.C.

And in Bithynia (now northern Asiatic Turkey) this coin of a king named Prusias (228-180 B.C.) was struck. It, too, is a tetradrachm. It might be recalled that Bithynia was famous, or infamous, during the time of Julius Caesar, for Caesar had been harangued in the senate purportedly for misbehaving with the king of Bithynia.

The beautiful queen Arsinoe, wife of Ptolemy II (284-247 B.C.) appears upon this dekadrachm. Ptolemy ruled over Egypt after the Alexandrine empire was distributed among Alexander's generals at his death.

King Eucratides of Bactria (200-150 B.C.) appears upon this tetradrachm struck during his rule. Present-day Afghanistan occupies the area which once was Bactria.

THE PERIOD OF CONTINUED DECLINE IN ART
(146-27 B.C.)

In this period, there is unquestionably a decline in the quality of the coinage. Generally, the period covers the span of time from the conquest of Greece by the Romans to the beginning of the Roman Empire under Augustus. Undoubtedly, forces brought to bear upon the Greeks precluded any effort of an artistic nature. Men were fighting for their lives, in addition to which coins were struck only with the sufferance of Rome. Now we find detail lacking upon the coinage, inspiration sags, and creativeness settles for a less lofty perch. There is an absence of realism noticeable, an air of haste of creation.

Pictured is a tetradrachm of Antiochus X of Syria (94-83 B.C.) and one of a contemporary, Phillipus Philadelphus of Syria (92-83 B.C.)

Moving into Numidia (now north Africa in the vicinity of present-day Tunis) we find a coin of Hiempsal II (106-60 B.C.)

From Egypt during the reign of Ptolemy X we have this coin (80-51 B.C.). This coin is also a tetradrachm.

Menander of Bactria struck this coin during his reign. (About 120 B.C.). It is a drachm.

This tetradrachm was issued by Mithradates II of Parthia (123-88 B.C.).

THE IMPERIAL PERIOD
(27 B.C.-A.D. 268)

This period actually is more Roman than Greek and the coinage is considered only because the inscriptions on them are in Greek. The years cover the period of time between the Emperor Augustus and the Emperor Gallienus. Most of the coins look exactly like the Roman Imperial coinage in that they carry the busts of the Emperors or members of the Imperial family upon them. For the most part, the coins are

35

local in character, minted by the various communities with Rome's approval. The minor satraps and petty rulers, most of whom were rulers in name only, probably felt obliged to place the Emperor's bust upon their coinage. Either this was a means of insuring a relatively healthy existence, or it was ordered that they do so. In any event the coinage certainly does not have the great merit of those coins issued during the peak age of Greek coin-art.

Antioch, in Pisidia (now Turkey), struck this bronze coin with the image of Septimius Severus upon it. Severus ruled from A.D. 193 to 211.

Caracalla appears upon this large bronze coin struck in Tabae, Caria (western Turkey). He was Emperor from A.D. 211 to 217.

The Emperor Trajan Decius appears upon this coin struck in Ionia by the community of Ephesus. He ruled Rome from A.D. 249-251.

The inept and degraded Commodus, son of the noble Marcus Aurelius, appears upon this coin struck at Kyzicus, in Mysia (also Turkey). Commodus ruled from A.D. 180 to 192. His rule ended when he was strangled to death at the age of 31.

The Imperial Period brings to an end the coinage of anything that is Greek. Rome has reached its height and also has begun to fall. Greece has become merely an element of the Empire and never again shall it be among the world powers. Yet, anyone familiar with history is thoroughly aware that Greece has never died. Nothing dies that leaves such a heritage. Today we live under Greek influence as assuredly as if we had lived in those days.

In conclusion, it should be apparent in examining this section that many of these periods seem to overlap, that coins might be placed into one or another of the periods. This is unavoidable, for the art did not grow simultaneously throughout the Greek world. During the period of the Decline of the Art, we have already noted that there was not too serious a decline in the coinage of Asia Minor, yet the coinage in the European part of the Greek world did evidence a decline.

AN ALPHABETICAL LIST OF THE COINS
OF THE GREEK WORLD

Constant referral to this section should provide a reasonable aid to the identification and classification of the coins of the Greek world. The list is by no means complete. However, each city listed is represented by an illustration of one of its coins. Inasmuch as hundreds of illustrations appear, the reader will find an excellent cross section, his own library so to speak, to which he may refer. Very few collectors would be able to gather the great number of coins shown here, yet the general excellence of the photographs will provide a laboratory of familiarization. Certain salient facts are contained in this section to make identification easier. The reader will see the following:

1. The illustrated coin.
2. Identification of the figures on the obverse and reverse of the coin shown.

3. The name of the city upon the coin. If the coin does not bear the name of the city, the name is listed, nevertheless, as it would appear in Greek.
4. The translation of the name.
5. The name of the modern town at the location, if there is a modern town.
6. The location of the town.
7. The approximate date the illustrated coin was struck.

The seven points of information just noted appear in a lesser number of columns in the interest and necessity of space conservation.

It should always be born in mind that the illustrated coin is but one of many struck in any particular community. Any attempt to present illustrations of all the coins struck in ancient Greece obviously would be an impossible task, certainly insofar as the intent of this book is concerned. Let the reader not despair, then, if his own coin is not illustrated. If the name of a town appears upon his coin he may be able to identify it by examining the listing of the names.

A word about those cities which are not shown in this chart. In order to locate the photographs which have been incorporated into this section, and throughout this book as well, it was necessary to spend many months searching through catalogs, some of which dated back 30 to 35 years. It was felt that if an illustration was not to be found in these countless catalogs, it was absent either because of its great rarity or its insignificance. In either case, such coins would not normally pass through the hands of the reader of this book and, therefore, the mere listing of the town without an illustration would be superfluous.

If, in certain instances, the dating of a coin seems to cover a very broad period, it must be remembered that the study of Greek coinage is not exact. Dating something more than 2000 years old is a prodigious task indeed. Rather, it is remarkable that so many of the coins have been dated with a high degree of accuracy. This is why classical numismatics and archaeology are inseparable. Before we can begin to date the coin, it must be dug up and the area from which it has been taken must be analyzed with painstaking care. Other items found with the coins, potsherds, or fragments, must all tie in before experts may be able to stamp some authenticity of date upon the subject in question. Much of this has been done. Much remains to be done. This is the fascination which grasps and holds those fortunate enough to find such study a part of their lives.

It should also be remembered that the symbols or inscriptions upon the coins do not always indicate the name of the city by which they were struck. Sometimes much more was put upon the coins, such as magistrates' names and inscriptions, which baffle scholars today. It should also be noted that the names of the cities in Greek, as they are listed in this section, may be the full name, or a foreshortened one. Syracuse, for example, and one example out of many, may appear as ΣΥΡΑΚ, ΣΥΡΑ, ΣΥΡΑΚΟΣΙΩΝ or even as ΕΣΡ. If this is kept in mind when examining the illustrations or the reader's own coins, his task will be considerably less difficult.

In conclusion, as a general rule for broad periods of dating, those coins which have incuse reverses and those which have the depressed replica of the obverse upon the reverse are the older Greek coins, simply because the Greeks started to strike coins such as these, having no interest in placing the figures and other symbols upon the coins until a later period.

GUIDE TO SYMBOLS AND CITY NAMES

Griffin—Apollo

NAME OF TOWN Translation Modern Name, If Any	LOCATION	DATE OF COIN
ΑΒΔΗΡΙΤΕΩΝ Abdera	South coast of upper Greece in Thrace, on the Aegean Sea	408-350 B.C.

![Lucius Verus—Hercules coin]

Lucius Verus—Hercules

ΑΒΙΛΗΝΩΝ Abila Abil	Southeast of Sea of Galilee in Palestine	A.D. 221

Artemis—Eagle

ΑΒΥΔΗΝΩΝ Abydus	At the Dardanelles, Turkey in Asia	196 B.C.

Bull Kneeling—Incuse Square

NAME OF TOWN
Translation
Modern Name, If Any | LOCATION | DATE OF COIN

AKANΘION
Acanthus | On the Chalcidian peninsula above Acte, Macedonia | 500-424 B.C.

Achelous—Apollo

AKAPNANΩN
Acarnania | An ancient country on the west coast of Greece above the Peloponnesus facing the island of Cephalonia. | 250-167 B.C.

River God—Belos

AKH
Ace (also Ptolemais-Ace)
Acre | Then in Phoenicia. Now on coast of Israel | A.D. 250

Zeus—Achaean Monogram

AXAIΩN
Achaean | Coinage of the Achaean league, the cities of the northeast Peloponnesus of Greece | 280-200 B.C.

Gallienus—Artemis

NAME OF TOWN Translation Modern Name, If Any	LOCATION	DATE OF COIN
AKMONEΩN *Acmoneia*	In Phrygia, now part of Turkey, 150 miles inland from west coast	A.D. 253-268

Shield—Kantharos

AK *Acraephia*	In Boeotia, Greece, about 50 miles northwest of Athens	456-446 B.C.

Herennius—Nike

AΔAΔEΩN *Adada* Karabaulo	In ancient Pisidia, now a part of Turkey about 50 miles north of Antalya	A.D. 249-251

Snake Coming Out of Basket—2 Snakes

AΔPAMYTHNΩN *Adramyteum* Edremit	In Mysia, now that part of Turkey encompassing the Bay of Edremit	133-67 B.C.

He Goat—Incuse Square

AIΓAEΩN *Aegae* Edessa	Original capitol of Macedonia (northern Greece)	500-480 B.C.

Land Tortoise—Incuse Square

NAME OF TOWN Translation Modern Name, If Any	LOCATION	DATE OF COIN
ΑΙΓΙΝΑ *Aegina*	An island in the Saronikon Gulf, south of Athens	404-340 B.C.

Head of Zeus—Achaean Monogram

ΑΙΓΙΕΩΝ *Aegium* Agion	In Achaia, northern part of Grecian Peloponnesus	280-146 B.C.

Demeter—Goat

ΑΙΓΟΣΓΟ *Aegospotami*	On the Thracian peninsula	300 B.C.

Antoninus Pius—City Goddess

AEL KAP *Aelia Capitolina* Jerusalem	In present-day Palestine	A.D. 138-161

Head of Aeneas—Incuse Square

ΑΙΝΕΙΑΤΩΝ *Aeneia*	In Macedonia, west side of Chal- cidian peninsula	500-424 B.C.

42

Head of Athena—Slinger

Hermes—Goat

AINION
Aenus
Enez

In Thrace, now Turkey in Europe.
At mouth of Hebrus River

400-350 B.C.

Italia—Soldiers

AIƧERNINO
Aesernia
Isernia

Central Samnium, in Italy

90-88 B.C.

Male Head—Spearhead and Jawbone

AITΩΛΩN
Aetolia

In south-central Greece just
above Peloponnesus

279-168 B.C.

Augustus—Zeus and Eagle

AIZANITΩN
Aezania

In Phrygia, now Turkey, near
source of Rhyndacus River

34 B.C.-A.D. 14

Crab—Eagle

NAME OF TOWN		
Translation		
Modern Name, If Any	LOCATION	DATE OF COIN
AKPAΓANTOΣ	South-central coast of Sicily	427-413 B.C.
Acragas or Agrigentum		
Agrigento		

Eagle—Spokes and Wheel

AΓYPINAION
Agyrium
Agira

The interior of Sicily   420-345 B.C.

Apollo—Pegasos

AΛABANΔEΩN
Alabanda

In ancient Caria, now southwest
Turkey   197-189 B.C.

Hermes—Griffin

AⱢBA
Alba Fucens

In Latium, central Italy   280-263 B.C.

Apollo—Kithara

AΛEΞANΔPEΩN
Alexandreia Troas
Eski Stambul

In the vicinity of ancient Troy,
now northwest Turkey in Asia   Before 189 B.C.

Hadrian—Serapis

NAME OF TOWN Translation Modern Name, If Any	LOCATION	DATE OF COIN
ALEXANDRIA (Name does not appear on coins)	In Egypt	A.D. 117-138

Apollo—Skylla and Shell

| ΑΛΛΙΒΑΝΟΝ
Alliba
Alife | In Campania, Italy, east side of
Vulturnus valley | 350 B.C. |

Pegasos—Athena

| ΑΛΥΙΑΙΩΝ
Alyzia | West coast of Greece, northeast
of island of Cephalonia | 350-250 B.C. |

Phyrigian—Female Holding Nike

| ΑΜΑΣΤΡΙΕΩΝ
Amastris
Amasra | In ancient Paphlagonia now in
Turkey, on Black Sea | 300 B.C. |

Lion—Lion and Eagle

| *Amathus* | On the island of Cyprus | 450-400 B.C. |

Dione—Obelisk

NAME OF TOWN Translation Modern Name, If Any	LOCATION	DATE OF COIN
AMBPA *Ambracia*	In Epirus, west Greece, opposite island of Corcyra	238-168 B.C.

Dionysos—Cista and Thyrsos

AMIΣOY Amisus *Eski Samsun*	On Black Sea coast in ancient Pontus now Turkey	100 B.C.

Apollo—Dolphin

AMφΓOΛITEΩN *Amphipolis*	In Macedonia on Strymon River near coast	424-358 B.C.

Pegasos—Athena

ANAKTOPIΩN *Anactorium*	In Arcarnania, southwest corner of middle Greece	350-300 B.C.

Reverse, Prize Crowns

ANAZAPBEΩN Anazarbus *Anavarza*	In Cilicia, now southern Turkey, along coast	A.D. 253-260

Gordianus and Tranquillina—Artemis

NAME OF TOWN Translation Modern Name, If Any		
	LOCATION	DATE OF COIN
ANXIAΛEΩN *Anchialus*	In ancient Thrace, now Bulgaria	238-244 B.C.

Nerva—Temple

ANKVPA
Ancyra
Angora

In ancient Galatia, now central
Turkey

A.D. 96-98

Apollo—Lion's Head

ANTAN
Antandrus

In the ancient Troas, now in
Turkey, north coast of Bay of
Edremit

300 B.C.

Septimius Severus—Goddess

ANTIOCH
Antiocheia
Yalovadj

In ancient Pisidia, now south-
central Turkey

A.D. 193-211

47

Augustus—Tyche. The river god Orontes at her feet

NAME OF TOWN Translation Modern Name, If Any	LOCATION	DATE OF COIN
ANTIOXEΩN *Antiocheia ad Orontem* Antakya	In the northern part of Syria near the sea	29 B.C.—A.D. 14

Athena—Eagle

AΠAMEΩN *Apameia*	In ancient Phrygia, now west- central Turkey	57-53 B.C.

Gordianus III—Centaur

AΦPOΔIΣIEΩN *Aphrodisias*	In Caria, now west Turkey	A.D. 238-244

Winged Figure—Cone in Incuse

Aphrodisias	In ancient Cilicia, now southern coast of Turkey	485-425 B.C.

Apollo—Amphora

NAME OF TOWN		
Translation		
Modern Name, If Any	LOCATION	DATE OF COIN
ΑΠΛΛΩΝΟΣ	In Macedonia, Greece	300-200 B.C.
Apollonia		

Gorgon Head—Crayfish and Anchor

ΑΠΟΛΛΩΝΟΣ   In Thrace, now Bulgaria, on Black   450-330 B.C.
Apollonia   Sea
Sozopolis

Athena—Obelisk

ΑΓΟΛΛΩΝΙΑΤΑΝ   In Illyricum, now Yugoslavia   1st century B.C.
Apollonia

Severus Alexander—Goddess Sacrificing

ΑΠΟΛΛΩΝΙΑΤΩΝ   In ancient Mysia, now northwest   A.D. 222-235
Apollonia   Turkey
Abulliont

Septimius Severus—Hygieia and Asklepios

ΑΠΟΛΛΩΝΙΑΤΩΝ   In ancient Pisidia, now south-   A.D. 193-211
Apollonia   west Turkey
Oluburlu

Artemis—Armed Warrior

NAME OF TOWN Translation Modern Name, If Any	LOCATION	DATE OF COIN
ΑΓΤΕΡΑΙΩΝ *Aptera*	On the northeast coast of Crete	400-300 B.C.

Tyche—Nike

ΑΡΑΔΙΩΝ *Arados*	On an island off the coast of ancient Phoenicia, now probably modern Lebanon	137-46 B.C.

Pan—Syrinx

APK *Arkadia*	Central Peloponnesos in Greece	370-363 B.C.

Pegasos—Athena

ΑΡΓΕΙΩΝ *Argos Amphilochicum*	In ancient Acarnania, now south- west corner of Greek mainland	350-300 B.C.

Hera—Dolphin

ΑΡΓΕΙΩΝ *Argos*	Northeast part of Peloponnesus in Greece	421-350 B.C.

Galloping Horse—Hook and Ring

NAME OF TOWN Translation Modern Name, If Any		DATE OF COIN
ΑΡΓΑΝΩΝ *Arpi* Arpa	LOCATION In Apulia, southeast Italy	300-200 B.C.

Bearded Head—Horse

NO INSCRIPTION
Arverni

An ancient Gallic tribe probably
in Spain or France

Middle of 1st
century B.C.

Hadrian—Dove, Stag, Goddess

ΑCΚΑΛ-N
Ascalon

In ancient Judaea, now the coast
of Israel

A.D. 117-138

Wrestlers—Slinger

ΕΣΤΦΕΔΙΙΥΣ
(Pamphylian for
ΑCΠΕΝΔΙΩΝ)
Aspendus
Balkyzi

In ancient Pamphylia, now southern
Turkey on Mediterranean

400-300 B.C.

Athena—Owl

ΑΘΕ
Athens

In Attica, Greece

220-197 B.C.

51

Goddess—Athena

NAME OF TOWN
Translation
Modern Name, If Any

LOCATION

DATE OF COIN

ATTAITΩN
Attaea

In ancient Mysia, now northwest Turkey

A.D. 98-217

Livia—Ram

AYΓOYCTA-NΩN
Augusta

In ancient Cilicia, now south Turkey
just above Syria

About A.D. 20

Head of Apollo—Tripod

A≡ IΩN
Axus (also Naxus)

On the island of Crete north of
Mt. Ida

4th century B.C.

Zeus—Silphium

BAPKEΣIOΣ
Barce

In what is now Libya, Africa

431-321 B.C.

Macrinus—Eagle

BЄPOIAIΩN
Beroea
Haleb (or Aleppo)

In ancient Cyrrhestica, now Syria

A.D. 217-218

Macrinus—Temple

| NAME OF TOWN Translation Modern Name, If Any | LOCATION | DATE OF COIN |

NAME OF TOWN
Translation
Modern Name, If Any

BER
Berytus
Beyrout

LOCATION
In ancient Phoenicia, now Lebanon

DATE OF COIN
A.D. 217-218

Warrior with 2 Spears—Incuse Square

ΒΙΣΑΛΤΙΚΟΝ
(Retrograde Inscription)
Bisaltae

An ancient Macedonian tribe
in the vicinity of the Strymon
River

About 500 B.C.

Sabina—Temple

ΒΕΙΘΥΝΙΑC
Bithynia

A country along southern shore
of Black Sea, now Turkey

A.D. 117-138

Philip—Asklepios and Hygieia

ΒΙΖVΗΝΩΝ
Bizya

In Thrace, now Turkey in Europe

A.D. 244-249

Nero—Apollo

NAME OF TOWN		
Translation		
Modern Name, If Any	LOCATION	DATE OF COIN

BΛAYNΔ∈ΩN
Blaundus
Suleimanli

In Lydia, now Turkey, on Hippurius River

A.D. 54-68

Shield—Amphora

BOIΩTΩN
Boeotia

A section of ancient Greece above Athens

338-315 B.C.

Commodus—Deity(?)

BOSTRA
Bostra

In Arabia about 70 miles south of Damascus (Syria)

A.D. 180-192

Shield—Ship's Prow

BOTTEATΩN
Bottiaea

A district in Macedonia, Greece

185-168 B.C.

Ares—Bellona

BPETTIΩN
Bruttium

The toe of Italy

282-203 B.C.

Athena—Grain

NAME OF TOWN Translation Modern Name, If Any	LOCATION	DATE OF COIN
BYTONTINΩN Butuntum Bitonto	In Apulia, Italy, near coast	3rd century B.C.

Diadumenian—Astarte in Temple

BVBΛOV Byblus Jubeil	Ancient Phoenician coast town, now in Lebanon	A.D. 217-218

Cow Standing on Dolphin—Incuse Square

Γ = B Byzantium	Present-day Istanbul at the Bosporus, Turkey, in Europe	416-357 B.C.

Reverse Only, Nike

KABHPΩN Cabeira Niksar	In ancient Pontus, now that part of Turkey which borders the Black Sea	Around 100 B.C.

Sabina—Artemis

KAΔOHNΩN Cadi Gediz	In Phrygia, now Turkey	A.D. 117-138

Nerva—Tyche

NAME OF TOWN Translation Modern Name, If Any	LOCATION	DATE OF COIN
KAICAPE ω N *Caerarea* Kaisariyeh	In Cappadocia, now eastern part of Turkey	A.D. 96-98

Steer—4-Part Square

| KAΛX
Calchedon
Kadikeui | Ancient Bithynia, the Black Sea
coastal region of present-day
Turkey | 412-394 B.C. |

· Athena—Nike in Biga

| CALENO
Cales
Calvi | In Campanian district of Italy | 280-268 B.C. |

Male Head—Lyre

| KAΛYMNION
Calymna | An island off the coast of Turkey
in the Sporades group. Formerly
ancient Caria | 3rd century B.C. |

Quadriga—Herakles

| KAMAPINAION
Kamarina | On the south coast of Sicily | 420-413 B.C. |

Fig Leaf—Incuse Square

NAME OF TOWN Translation Modern Name, If Any	LOCATION	DATE OF COIN
KAMIPEΩN *Kamiros*	On the west coast of the island of Rhodes	6th century B.C.

Zeus—Nike

| USUALLY ROMANO
Capua | In the Campanian district of Italy | 280-268 B.C. |

Amphora—Incuse Square

| KAPΘAI
Karthaia | On the southeast coast of the island of Keos in the Aegean | 500-480 B.C. |

Persephone—Head of Horse

| *Carthage* | Famous city in ancient Zeugitana, now Tunisia in Africa. Near present-day Tunis | 410-310 B.C. |

Tiberius—Nero and Drusus

| *Carthago Nova* | In present-day Spain | A.D. 14-37 |

Herakles—Steer

NAME OF TOWN
Translation
Modern Name, If Any   LOCATION   DATE OF COIN
ΚΑΡΙΣΤΩΝ   Southern part of the division of   387-369 B.C.
Karystos   Euboia in Greece

Severus Alexander—Athena

ΚΑCΑΤΩΝ   In ancient Cilicia, southeastern   A.D. 222-235
Casae   part of present-day Turkey

Apollo—Quadriga

ΚΑΤΑΝΑΙΟΝ   East-central Sicily at base of Mt. Aetna   420-413 B.C.
Katane
Catania

Male Figure—Incuse

ΚΑΥΛ   Was on the east coast of the division   550-480 B.C.
Kaulonia   of Brutium in Italy

Lion—Incuse Square

K̄ AY   In ancient Caria, now Turkey,   About 500 B.C.
Kaunos   opposite Rhodes

Ram's Head—Incuse Square

NAME OF TOWN Translation Modern Name, If Any	LOCATION	DATE OF COIN
KEBRENE *Kebren*	On the Troas, northwestern Turkey	6th century B.C.

Horseman—Goat

| KEΛEN *Kelenderis* Tchelindre | Ancient Cilicia, now southeastern Turkey opposite island of Cyprus | 400-350 B.C. |

Zeuz—Thunderbolt

| KENTOPIΓINΩN *Kentaripai* Centorbi | On the island of Sicily | About 241 B.C. |

Quadriga—Arethusa

| KEΦAΛOIΔIOY *Kephaloidion* Cefalu | Northern coast of Sicily | 409-396 B.C. |

Artemis—Club

| KЄPAЄITΩN *Keraitai* | In ancient Pisidia, now south-central Turkey | About 100 B.C. |

City Goddess—Galloping Horseman

NAME OF TOWN Translation Modern Name, If Any	LOCATION	DATE OF COIN
KAPKI *Carcine*	On the Tauric peninsula, Black Sea area, now part of Soviet Russia	About 300 B.C.

Apollo—Lyre

ΧΑΛΚΙΔΕΩΝ Chalkidian League	The peninsula district of Macedonia, Greece. Minted at Olynthos a colony of Chalkis	392-358 B.C.

Arethusa—Eagle

ΧΑΛΚΙΔΕΩΝ *Chalkis*	Famous Ionian town in the division of Euboea in Greece	340-294 B.C.

Artemis—Stag

XEP *Cherronesos*	In ancient times, on the Tauric Chersonesos, now near Sebastopol in Russia	3rd century B.C.

Athena—Ship's Prow

ΧΕΡΣΟΝΑΣΙΩΝ *Chersonesos* *Chersoneso*	On the north coast of Crete	300-220 B.C.

Lion—Bull

NAME OF TOWN Translation Modern Name, If Any	LOCATION	DATE OF COIN
XEP *Cherronesos*	In ancient Caria, now west Turkey	550-500 B.C.

Sphinx—Amphora

| XIOΣ
Chios | One of the largest of the Aegean Islands. Also the name of its principal town on east coast | About 84 B.C. |

Zeus—Club

| XΩM
Choma | In Lycia, now southeast Turkey | About 100 B.C. |

Male Head—Rider

| KIBYPATΩN
Cibyra | In ancient Phrygia, now west-central Turkey | 166-84 B.C. |

Zeus—Arne

| KIEPIEIΩN
Cierium
Thessaliotis | In Thessaly, upper Greece | 400-344 B.C. |

Herakles—Lion

| Cypriat inscription
Citium
Larnaka | On the island of Cyprus | 449-425 B.C. |

Apollo—Prow of Ship

NAME OF TOWN Translation Modern Name, If Any	LOCATION	DATE OF COIN
KIANΩN *Cius* Ghemlik	In ancient Bithynia, now Turkey, on the Sea of Marmara near the Bosporus	330-302 B.C.

Winged Boar's Head—Incuse Square

KΛA *Clazomenae*	In Ionia, now westernmost Turkey on the Bay of Izmir	545-494 B.C.

Athena—Horse

KΛH *Cleitor*	In Arcadia, central Peloponnesus, Greece	400-322 B.C.

Lion—Aphrodite

KNIΔION *Knidos*	In Caria, now southwestern part of Turkey	650-480 B.C.

Hera—Labyrinth

KNΩΣION *Knosos*	On the island of Crete	350-220 B.C.

Apollo—Lyre

NAME OF TOWN
Translation
Modern Name, If Any

LOCATION

DATE OF COIN

KOΛΟΦΩΝΙΩΝ
Kolophon

In Ionia, now the western shore
of Turkey

About 350 B.C.

Shield with Gorgon—Nike

KOMANΩN
Komana

Was located in ancient Pontus,
now Turkey, south shore of Black sea

About 100 B.C.

Cow Suckling Calf—Patterns in Two Squares

KOP
Corcyra

An island off the west coast of
central Greece

525-500 B.C.

Cuttlefish—Incuse Square

KOPH
Koressia

On the island of Keos in the
Aegean

600-480 B.C.

Pegasos—Athena

KOPINΘΙΩΝ
Corinth

On the Grecian Peloponnesus at
eastern end of Gulf of Corinth

400-338 B.C.

Boeotian Shield—Gorgon Head

| NAME OF TOWN
Translation
Modern Name, If Any
KOP
Koroneia | LOCATION
In the division of Boeotia, above
the Attic peninsula in Greece | DATE OF COIN
456-446 B.C. |

Pegasos—Athena

| K
Koronta | In Arkarnania, southwestern
Greek mainland | 300-250 B.C. |

Otacilia Severa—Tyche

| KΩPVA
Corycus
Korgos | In Cilicia, now southeastern Turkey | A.D. 244-249 |

Herakles—Crab

| KΩION
Kos | An island in the Aegean off ancient
Caria, now Turkey | 300-190 B.C. |

Female Head—Wreath

| Semitic inscription
Cossura
Pantelleria | An island between Sicily and
Africa | About 217 B.C. |

Ram's Head—Animal's Hoof

NAME OF TOWN Translation Modern Name, If Any	LOCATION	DATE OF COIN
KPA *Cranium*	An island off the coast of Elis, western Peloponnesus, Greece	About 400 B.C.

Tranquillina—Artemis

| CREMNA *Cremma* Girme | Ancient Pisidia, now west and south of central Turkey | A.D. 238-244 |

Zeus—Tyche (or Hera?)

| KPΩMNA *Cromma* | A city in ancient Paphlagonia, now northern Turkey near Black Sea | 340-300 B.C. |

Hera—Herakles

| QPO *Kroton* | A city in the division of Bruttium, Italy | About 480 B.C. |

Nymph's Head—Mussel

| KYMAION *Cumae* | The oldest Greek colony on the west coast of Italy. In the Campanian district | 480-423 B.C. |

Artemis—Artemis

| NAME OF TOWN
Translation
Modern Name, If Any	LOCATION	DATE OF COIN
KYΔΩNIATAN
Cydonia
Khania | On the north coast and west end
of the island of Crete | 200-67 B.C. |

Hermes—Two-handled vase

KYΨE
Kypsela
Ipsala

Situated near Aimos in northern
Greece

About 480 B.C.

Kyme—Horse

KYMAIΩN
Cyme
Namourt

In ancient Aeolis, now that part
of Turkey opposite the island of
Mytilene

About 190 B.C.

Vespasian—Temple Front

KY
Cyprus

An island at the east end of the
Mediterranean

A.D. 69-79

Quadriga—Zeus

NAME OF TOWN Translation Modern Name, If Any	LOCATION	DATE OF COIN
KYPANAION *Kyrene* Cirene	On the coast of north Africa west of Egypt	431-321 B.C.

Herakles—Incuse Square

KYI *Kyzicus*	On the southern shore of the Sea of Mamara, Turkey	6th century B.C.

Septimius Severus—City God

ΔAMACK *Damascus*	In Syria	A.D. 193-211

Apollo—Tripod

ΔAMAΣTINΩN Damastium	In Illyrium, now Yugoslavia	4th century B.C.

Ram's Head—Goat's Head

DAΛ *Delphi*	In the division of Phocis, southern Greek mainland	520-480 B.C.

Hera Synkletos—Tyche

NAME OF TOWN
Translation
Modern Name, If Any

LOCATION

DATE OF COIN

ΔΟΚΙΜΕΩΝ
Docimeium
Ichje Kara-hissar

In ancient Phrygia, now west-central Turkey

2nd century A.D.

Gordian III and Serapis—Demeter

ΔΥΙΟΝΥ
Dionysopolis

In the Danube district called South Moesia

A.D. 238-244

Trajan—Astarte

ΔΩ ΡΙΤΩ Ν
Dora
Tantura

In ancient Phoenicia, now Israel

A.D. 98-117

Reverse, Cybele

ΔΟΡΥΛΑΕΩΝ
Dorylaeum
Eski-shehr

West-central Turkey, formerly ancient Phrygia

A.D. 222-235

Cow Suckling Calf — Double Stellate Square

NAME OF TOWN Translation Modern Name, If Any	LOCATION	DATE OF COIN
ΔΥΡ *Dyrrhachium*	Now Yugoslavia, formerly ancient Illyricum	4th century B.C.

Pegasos — Athena with Fish Hook

E *Echinus*	In ancient Acarnania, now southwest Greek mainland	300-250 B.C.

Caracalla — City God

ΕΔΕCCA *Edessa*	Now a part of Iraq, formerly Mesopotamia	A.D. 211-217

Goose — Incuse Square

Eion	In Macedonia, northern Greece	500-437 B.C.

Triptolemos — Boar

ΕΛΕΥΣΙ *Eleusis*	On the Attic peninsula in Greece, above Athens	339-322 B.C.

Apollo — Apollo

NAME OF TOWN		
Translation		
Modern Name, If Any	LOCATION	DATE OF COIN

ΕΛΕΥΘΕΡΝΑΙΟΝ
Eleutherna

In the interior of the island of Crete

431-300 B.C.

Septimius Severus — City God

ΕΛΕΥΘΕ
Eleutheropolis

Located in ancient Judea, about
20 miles from present-day Jerusalem

A.D. 193-211

Zeus — Eagle

ΓΑΛΕΙΩΝ
Elis

In the division of Achaia, northern
Peloponnesus, Greece

323-300 B.C.

Goat — Bee

ΕΛΥΡΙΟΝ
Elyrus
Rhodhovani

In southwestern Crete

400-300 B.C.

Female Figure — Man-Headed Bull

NAME OF TOWN
Translation
Modern Name, If Any

LOCATION

DATE OF COIN

ENTEΛ
Entella
Rocca d'Entella

On the island of Sicily

About 450 B.C.

Zeus — Eagle

ΑΓΕΙΡΩΤΑΝ
Epirus

In ancient Epirus, now Albania

233-168 B.C.

Artemis — Stag

ΕΦ
Ephesus

In ancient Ionia, now western Turkey

258-202 B.C.

Nymph — Steer Head

ΕRΕΤΡΙΕΩΝ
Eretria

In the division of Euboea in Greece

369-336 B.C.

Herakles — Club and Quiver

ΕΡΥ
Erythrae

Western Turkey, formerly ancient
Ionia

387-300 B.C.

Geta — Apollo(?)

NAME OF TOWN
Translation
Modern Name, If Any

ЄΤЄΝΝЄ ⲱ Ν
Etenna

LOCATION

Was located in Pisidia, now
south-central Turkey

DATE OF COIN

A.D. 209-212

Maximinus and Maximus, Obverse

EYKAPΠITIKOY
Eucarpeia
Emir Hissar

In ancient Phrygia, now central
Turkey

A.D. 306-307

Agrippina the Younger — Cybele

EYMENEΩN
Eumeneia
Ishekli

In ancient Phrygia, now central
Turkey

Middle of 1st
century A.D.

Antoninus Pius — Men Standing

ΓABHNΩN
Gaba

In Trachonitis, now Latakia

A.D. 138-161

Marcus Aurelius — Temple

NAME OF TOWN
Translation
Modern Name, If Any

ΓΑΔΑΡΕωΝ
Gadara
Umm Keis

LOCATION
In Decapolis, now Trans-Jordan

DATE OF COIN
A.D. 161-180

Trajan — Temple

ΓΑΛΑΤΙΑΣ
Galatia

An ancient country, now central Turkey

A.D. 98-117

Herakles — Incluse

NO INSCRIPTION
Gallia

That area which encompasses much
of the western part of Europe

520-470 B.C.

Athena — Owl

ΓΑΖΑ
Gaza

In ancient Judea, now Israel

425-400 B.C.

Biga — Man-Headed Bull

ΓΕΛΑΣ
Gela
Terranova

On the Island of Sicily

Before 466 B.C.

Sybil — Sphinx

NAME OF TOWN
Translation
Modern Name, If Any
ΓΕΡ
Gergis

LOCATION
Northwestern Turkey, formerly
the Troad

DATE OF COIN
400-350 B.C.

Gordian III — Herakles on Lion
ΓЄΡΜΗΝΩΝ   In Lydia, now western Turkey   A.D. 238-244
Germe

Lion — Bull
Golgi(?)   On the island of Cyprus   About 450 B.C.

Nymph—Zeus
ΓΟΜΦΕΩΝ   In Thessaly, Greece   About 300 B.C.
Gomphi (also Philippopolis)
Histiaeotis

Europa — Bull

NAME OF TOWN		
Translation		
Modern Name, If Any	LOCATION	DATE OF COIN
ΓΟΡΤΥΝΙΩΝ	On the island of Crete	431-300 B.C.
Gortyna		

Commodus — Youth on Horse

ΑΔΡΙΑΝΟΠΟΛΕΙΤΩΝ   In Thrace, Greece   A.D. 180-192
Hadrianopolis

Shield — Incuse

ΑΛΙ   In the division of Boeotia in   550-480 B.C.
Haliartus(?)   Greece

Helios — Athena

ΑΛΙΚΑΡΝΑΣΣΕΩΝ   In Caria, now western Turkey   188-166 B.C.
Halicarnassus

Anchor — Value Number

NAME OF TOWN
Translation
Modern Name, If Any

HAT
Hatria
Atri

LOCATION
In the Umbrian division of Italy

DATE OF COIN
About 289 B.C.

Julia Domna — Eagle

HEL
Heliopolis
Baalbek

In Syria

1st part of 3rd
century A.D.

Demeter — Ethnic within incuse square

ER
Heraea

In Arcadia, central Peloponnesus,
Greece

550-490 B.C.

Athena — Hercules

ΗΡΑΚΛΕΙΩΝ
Heraclea
Policoro

In the division of Lucania, in the
arch of the foot of Italy

370-281 B.C.

Lion's Head — Club

NAME OF TOWN Translation Modern Name, If Any HPAK *Heracleia Trachinia* Oelaea	LOCATION In Thessaly, northern Greece	DATE OF COIN 400-344 B.C.

Dionysos — Herakles

HPAKΛEIA Heracleia Pontica *Benderegli*	In ancient Bithynia, south coast of Black Sea, now Turkey	345-337 B.C.

Athena — Club

HPAKΛ∈ΩTΩN *Heracleia ad Latmum*	In western Turkey, formerly ancient Ionia. On the Latmic Gulf	About 190 B.C.

Nero — Club

HPAKΛ∈ΩTΩN *Heracleia Salbace*	In ancient Caria, now western Turkey	A.D. 54-68

Demeter — Corn Wreath

EP *Hermione*	In Argolis on the Grecian Peloponnesus	350-322 B.C.

Female Head — Eagle and Palm

NAME OF TOWN Translation Modern Name, If Any	LOCATION	DATE OF COIN
ΙΕΡΑΠΥΤΝΙΩΝ *Hierapytna* Gierapetra	On the southern coast of the island of Crete	About 200 B.C.

Otacilia Severa — Prize Garlands

ΙΕΡΑΠΟΛΕΙΤΩΝ
Hierapolis
Pambuk Kalesi

In ancient Phrygia, now west-central Turkey

A.D. 244-249

Commodus — Tyche and Commodus

ΙΕΡΟΠΟΛΙΤΩΝ
Hieropolis-Castabala
Budrum

In Cilicia, now southeastern Turkey

A.D. 180-192

Cock — Hen

NAME OF TOWN
Translation
Modern Name, If Any

HIMEPAION
Himera
Termini

LOCATION
On the north coast of the island
of Sicily

DATE OF COIN
About 480 B.C.

Hermes — Caduceus
In the division of Bruttium, Italy

ΕΙΓΩΝΙΕΩΝ
Hipponium
Bivona

192-89 B.C.

Maenad — Bull
In the division of Euboea in
Greece

ΙΣΤΙ
Histiaea

369-336 B.C.

Hercules — Asklepios
In ancient Lydia, now western
Turkey

ΥΠΑΙΠΗΝΩΝ
Hypaepa

?

Reverse, Hades in Quadriga

NAME OF TOWN
Translation
Modern Name, If Any

YPKANΩN
Hyrcanis

LOCATION
In ancient Lydia, now western
Turkey

DATE OF COIN
A.D. 180-192

Hera — Bull

YΔINA
Hyria

In the Campanian district of
Italy

420-340 B.C.

Dove — Dove

YPTAKINIΩN
Hyrtacina

On the southwestern part of
Crete

400-300 B.C.

Temple — Lulav

HEBREW
INSCRIPTION
Herodion

In Israel
(Bar Kokhba War)

A.D. 134-135

Athena — Athena Ilias

NAME OF TOWN Translation Modern Name, If Any	LOCATION	DATE OF COIN
ΙΛΙΑΔΟΣ *Ilium* Hissarlik	In ancient Troad, now northwestern Turkey in Asia	About 189 B.C.

Bearded Head — Herakles

ΙΡΗΝΟΠΟΛΙΤΩΝ *Irenopolis*	In southeastern Turkey, formerly ancient Cilicia	?

Septimius Severus — Severus on Horse

ICTPIHNΩN *Istrus*	In ancient Sarmatia, now a part of Russia	A.D. 193-211

Athena — Eagle

ΙΤΑΝΙΩΝ *Itanus*	On the eastern coast of Crete	500-400 B.C.

Zeus — Amphora in Garland

NAME OF TOWN
Translation
Modern Name, If Any
ΛΑ
Lacedaemon

LOCATION
Southern part of the Grecian
Peloponnesus

DATE OF COIN
250-146 B.C.

Dionysus — Amphora
In Thessaly, middle Greece

ΛΑΜΙΕΩΝ
Lamia
Phthiotis

400-344 B.C.

Forepart of Winged Horse — Incuse Squares
In ancient Mysia on the Hellespont,
now northwestern Turkey

ΛΑΜ
Lampsacus

500-450 B.C.

Domitia — Zeus
In central Turkey, formerly
ancient Phrygia

ΛΑΟΔΙΚΕΩΝ
Laodiceia ad Lycum

A.D. 81-96

Gorgon — Nike

NAME OF TOWN
Translation
Modern Name, If Any

LOCATION

DATE OF COIN

ΛΑΟΔΙΚΕΙΑΣ
Laodiceia
Ladik

South of the Black Sea in Turkey.
Formerly ancient Pontus

About 100 B.C.

Tyche — Zeus

ΛΑΟΔΙΚΕΩΝ
Laodiceia ad Mare
Latakiyeh

In Syria, formerly Seleucis and
Pieria

1st century B.C.

Aphrodite — Athena

Lapethus

On the island of Cyprus

About 480 B.C.

Female Head — Bull's Head

ΛΑΓΓΑΙΩΝ
Lappa
Argyropolis

An inland town of western Crete

400-300 B.C.

Athena — Horse

NAME OF TOWN
Translation
Modern Name, If Any

LOCATION

DATE OF COIN

ᒪADINOD
Larinum
Larino Vecchio

Coinage of the tribe known as
the Frentani who occupied the
area between Samnium and the
Adriatic in Italy

About 250 B.C.

Nymph — Horse
In Thessaly, middle Greece

ΛΑΡΙΣΑΙΩΝ
Larissa
Pelasgiotis

400-344 B.C.

Man-Headed Bull — Man-Headed Bull
In the division of Lucania in Italy

ΛΑΙΝΩΝ
Laus
Laino

500-450 B.C.

Biga — Lion's Head
About twenty miles northwest of
Syracuse, in Sicily

ΛΕΟΝΤΙΝΟΝ
Leontini
Lentini

500-466 B.C.

Persephone — Bull

NAME OF TOWN Translation Modern Name, If Any	LOCATION	DATE OF COIN
ΛE (Rare) Lesbos	One of the largest islands of the eastern Aegean, now called Mytilene	400-350 B.C.

Satyr and Nymph — Incuse Square
In Macedon, northern Greece

ΛΕΤΑΙΟΝ
(Retrograde Inscription)
Lete

530-480 B.C.

Aphrodite Aineias — Ship's Prow
In ancient Acarnania, now the
southwestern corner of the Greek mainland

ΛΕΥΚΑΔΙΩΝ
Leukas

After 167 B.C.

Domitian — Dionysos in Quadriga
In Syria

ΛΕΥΚΑΔΙΩΝ
Leukas

A.D. 81-96

Lions Head — Incuse Square

NAME OF TOWN Translation Modern Name, If Any	LOCATION	DATE OF COIN
ΛΙΝΔΙ Lindos	On the east coast of the island of Rhodos	520-500 B.C.

Hephaestos — Three Marks of Value

ΛΙΓΑΡΑΙΟΝ
Lipara

An island off the northwest coast
of Sicily

About 350 B.C.

Dove — Dove

ΛΙΣΙΩΝ
Lisus

Southwestern part of the island
of Crete

400-300 B.C.

Zeus — Eagle

ΛΟΚΡΩΝ
Locri Epizephyrii

In the division of Bruttium in
Italy

332-326 B.C.

Persephone — Ajax

NAME OF TOWN
Translation
Modern Name, If Any
OΓONTION
Locri Opuntii

LOCATION
In Greece, about 50 miles northwest
of Athens

DATE OF COIN
369-338 B.C.

Forepart of Boar — Triskeles
Southwestern part of Turkey

ΛYKIΩN
Lycia

520-480 B.C.

Lion and Bull Facing — Incuse Square
Western part of Turkey. Formerly
a country

Lydia

561-546 B.C.

Eagle — Boar's Head
Eastern part of central Crete

ΛYTTIΩN
or ΓVKTSON
Lyttus
Xyda

400-300 B.C.

Herrenius Etruscus — Tyche

NAME OF TOWN		
Translation		
Modern Name, If Any	LOCATION	DATE OF COIN
MAIONΩN	In Lydia which is now far-west-	A.D. 251
Maeonia	central Turkey	
Menne		

Artemis — Apollo

MAΓNHTΩN   In ancient Ionia, now far-western   190-133 B.C.
Magnesia   Turkey

Caligula — Germanicus and Agrippina

MAΓNHTΩN   In ancient Lydia, now far-western   A.D. 37-41
Magnesia ad Sipylum   Turkey

Zeus — Artemis

MAΓNHTΩN   In Thessaly, central Greece   197-146 B.C.
Magnetes

Gallienus — Serapis

NAME OF TOWN Translation Modern Name, If Any	LOCATION	DATE OF COIN
ΜΑΓΥΔ∈ΩΝ Magydus Laara	In ancient Pamphylia, now south coastal section of central Turkey	A.D. 253-268

Winged Figure — Swan

MAPΛOTAN
Mallus

Southeastern coastal section of
Turkey, formerly Cilicia

425-385 B.C.

Ares — Eagle

MAMEPTINΩN
Mamertini (also Zancle
and Messana)

A tribe which lived at the north-
eastern corner of the island of
Sicily

288-216 B.C.

Berenice(?) — Marathos

MAPAΘHNΩN
Marathus
Amrit

In ancient Phoenicia, now Lebanon

221-151 B.C.

Elagabalus and Julia Maesa — Nike

NAME OF TOWN Translation Modern Name, If Any	LOCATION	DATE OF COIN
ΜΑΡΚΙΑΝΟΠΟΛΕΙΤΩΝ *Marcianopolis*	Now in Russia on the Black Sea. Formerly in Moesiae Inferior	A.D. 218-222

Horse — Square with Grape Vines

ΜΑΡΩΝΙΤΕΩΝ *Maroneia*	In Thrace, Greece	450-400 B.C.

Apollo — Lyre

MA Masicytes	Southern and western part of Turkey, formerly Lycia	81-27 B.C.

Artemis — Lion

ΜΑΣΣΑ *Massalia* *Marseille*	In ancient Gaul, now in France	About 200 B.C.

Commodus — Pallas

NAME OF TOWN		
Translation		
Modern Name, If Any	LOCATION	DATE OF COIN

MACTAYP∈ITΩN
Mastaura

In western Turkey, formerly Lydia

A.D. 180-192

Zeus — Pan

MEΓ
Megalopolis

In Arcadia, central Grecian
Peloponnesus

234-146 B.C.

Apollo — Lyre

MEΓAPEΩN
Megara

On the peninsula leading to the
Peloponnesus from Attica in
Greece

307-243 B.C.

Pomegranate — Half Moon

MAΛIΩN
Melos

One of the Aegean Islands

500-416 B.C.

Silenos — Amphora

NAME OF TOWN Translation Modern Name, If Any	LOCATION	DATE OF COIN
MENΔAIΩN Mende	In Macedonia, Greece	424-358 B.C.

Philip and Otacilia — Asklepios

MEΣAMBPIANΩN Mesembria	On the Black Sea in Russia	A.D. 244-249

Pegaso — Athena

MEΣMAIΩN Mesma or Medma	In the division of Bruttium in Italy	About 350 B.C.

Demeter — Zeus

MEΣΣANIΩN Messene	Had been located in Messenia, southern Grecian Peloponnesus	About 330 B.C.

Demeter — Ear of Corn

META Metapontum	In the division of Lucania in Italy	330-300 B.C.

Bear — Athena

NAME OF TOWN Translation Modern Name, If Any	LOCATION	DATE OF COIN
MAΘVMNAION Methymna	On the north coast of the island of Lesbos (now Mytilene)	500-450 B.C.

Pegasos — Athena

MH
Metropolis

In ancient Acarnania, now western
Greece above Peloponnesus

300-250 B.C.

Caracalla — Caracalla and God

MHTPOΠOΛ∈ITΩN
Metropolis

Near the coast, western Turkey.
Formerly Ionia.

A.D. 211-217

Apollo — Lion

Miletus

A famous city in ancient Ionia,
now western Turkey

300-250 B.C.

Athena — Lion

NAME OF TOWN Translation Modern Name, If Any	LOCATION	DATE OF COIN
MOPΓANTINΩN *Morgantina*	On the island of Sicily	344-317 B.C.

Gorgon — Palm Tree

MOTYAION *Motya*	At the west coast of the island of Sicily	413-397 B.C.

Boeotian Shield — Fulmen

MY *Mycalessus*	In the division of Boeotia in Greece	387-384 B.C.

Septimius Severus and Julia Domna —
Apollo and Artemis

MYNΔIΩN *Myndus*	In southwest Turkey, formerly Caria	A.D. 193-211

Apollo — Kithara

MYPA *Myra*	In ancient Lycia, southern and western Turkey	Before 81 B.C.

Apollo — Apollo Walking

NAME OF TOWN Translation Modern Name, If Any	LOCATION	DATE OF COIN
MYPINAIΩN *Myrina* Kalabassary	In Aeolis, now northwestern Turkey	After 189 B.C.

Apollo — Mytilene

| MVTIΛHNAON
Mytilene | The principal city of the island
of Lesbos (now called Mytilene).
Located in the eastern Aegean. | 440-400 B.C. |

Nymph — Seleinos

| NAKONAION
Nacona | On the island of Sicily | About 400 B.C. |

Aphrodite — Dionysus

| NAΓIΔIKON
Nagidus
Boz Yazi | In ancient Cilicia, now south-
eastern Turkey | 379-374 B.C. |

Kantharos — Incuse Square

NAME OF TOWN Translation Modern Name, If Any	LOCATION	DATE OF COIN
NA≡IΩN Naxos	One of the largest islands of the Cyclades group in the south- western Aegean Sea	600-490 B.C.

Dionysus — Grapes

NAXION
Naxus
Capo di Schiso

On the east coast of the island
of Sicily

Before 480 B.C.

Female Head — Man-Faced Bull

NEOΓOΛITΩN
Neapolis
Naples

In the Campanian district of Italy

300-241 B.C.

Gorgon — Incuse Square

NEOΓOΛITEΩN
Neapolis
Kavala

In Macedonia, Greece

510-480 B.C.

Marcus Aurelius — Jupiter Heliopolitanus

NAME OF TOWN Translation Modern Name, If Any	LOCATION	DATE OF COIN
NEAΠOΛ *Neapolis*	In ancient Samaria, now Palestine	A.D. 161-180

Augustus and Agrippa — Crocodile

NEM *Nemausus* Nimes	In Gaul, now France	Early 1st century A.D.

Faustina the Younger — Aphrodite

NIKOMHΔЄΩN *Nicomedia* Ismid	In northern Turkey near the western end of the Black Sea, formerly called Bithynia	A.D. 161-180

Diadumenian — Inscription

NIKOΠOΛЄITΩN *Nicopolis*	In Moesiae Inferior, now Romania	A.D. 217-218

Trajan — Zeus

NAME OF TOWN Translation Modern Name, If Any	LOCATION	DATE OF COIN
NINI *Ninica Claudiopolis*	In Cilicia, now southeastern Turkey	A.D. 98-117

Philip — God in Temple

NECIBI Nisibis	In Mesopotamia, now Iraq	A.D. 244-249

Nymph — Bull

NΩΛAIΩN Nola	In the Campanian district of Italy	340-325 B.C.

Male Head — One of the Dioscuri(?)

OSCAN INSCRIPTION *Nuceria Alfaterna*	In the Campanian district of Italy	280-268 B.C.

Elagabulus — Nike

NAME OF TOWN Translation Modern Name, If Any	LOCATION	DATE OF COIN
NYCAЄΩN *Nysa* Eski-Hissar	In Turkey, western portion, formerly Lydia	A.D. 218-222

Gordian III and Serapis — Hygiea

OΔHCCEITΩN
Odessus
Varna

In Moesiae Inferior, now Bulgaria   A.D. 238-244

Tiberius — Apollo

Oea
Tripoli

In ancient Syrtica, now Libya,   A.D. 14-37
North Africa

Lion's Head — Herakles

OITAIΩN
Oeta

In Thessaly, Greece   196-146 B.C.

Tiberius (Ajax) — Fulmen

NAME OF TOWN Translation Modern Name, If Any	LOCATION	DATE OF COIN
ΟΛΒΕΩΝ *Olba*	In southeastern Turkey, formerly Cilicia	A.D. 14-37

Athena — Shield

ΟΛΒΙΗ *Olbia*	In ancient Sarmatia, now Russia	300-100 B.C.

Athena — Thunderbolt

ΟΛΥΜΠΗ *Olympus*	In Lycia, now southern and eastern Turkey	About 100 B.C.

Apollo — Lyre

ΟΛ *Minted at Olynthus*	In the Chalcidian district of Macedonia in Greece	392-358 B.C.

Male Head — Artemis

ΕΡΧΟΜΕΝΙΩΝ *Orchomenos*	In the Arcadian district of the Peloponnesus, Greece	Middle of 4th century B.C.

Grain — Incuse Design

NAME OF TOWN Translation Modern Name, If Any	LOCATION	DATE OF COIN
EPXO *Orchomenos*	In the district of Boeotia in Greece	550-480 B.C.

Bull — Incuse Squares

ΩRHΣKIΩN
Orrescii

A people who occupied a
section of Macedonia

About 450 B.C.

Artemis — Helmet

OPΘAΓOPEΩN
Orthagoreia

In the Chalcidian district of
Macedonia in Greece

About 350 B.C.

Female Head — Kephalos

ΓA
Pale

On the island of Cephalonia off the
coast of Elis, western Peloponnesus, Greece

370-189 B.C.

Tripod — Bull

ΓANΔOΣIN
Pandosia

In the district of Bruttium in Italy

About 480 B.C.

Nymph — Dog

NAME OF TOWN Translation Modern Name, If Any	LOCATION	DATE OF COIN
ΓΑΝΟΡΜΙΤΙΚΟΝ Panormus *Palermo*	On the northwest coast of Sicily	480-409 B.C.

Dionysus — Garland

| ΓΑΝΤΙΚΑΠΑΙΤΩΝ *Panticapaeum* Kertch | On the Tauric peninsula, now Russia, on the Black Sea | About 250 B.C. |

Bull — Head of Eagle

| ΓΑΦΙ *Paphos* Kouklia | On the southwest coast of the island of Cyprus | About 460 B.C. |

Bull — Gorgon

| ΓΑΡΙ *Parium* Melde | In ancient Mysia, now northwestern Turkey | About 400 B.C. |

Male Head — Horse

| *Parisii* | A tribe which inhabited northern Gaul | 1st century B.C. |

Goat — Incuse Squares

NAME OF TOWN
Translation
Modern Name, If Any

LOCATION

DATE OF COIN

ΓΑΡΙ
Paros

On an island in the Cyclades
group in the Aegean

About 540 B.C.

Geta — Dionysus

ΠΑΥΤΑΛΙΩΤΩΝ
Pautalia

In Thrace, now Bulgaria

A.D. 209-212

Woman's Head — Table with Handle

ΠΕΛΑΓΙΤΩΝ
Pelagia

In Illyrium, now Yugoslavia

About 350 B.C.

Apollo — Laurel Wreath

ΓΕΛ
Pellene

In Achaia, northern Peloponnesus,
Greece

370-322 B.C.

Artemis — Artemis

ΠΕΡΓΑΙΑΣ
Perga
Murtana

In south-central Turkey, formerly
Pamphylia

About 190 B.C.

103

Commodus — Hygeia and Asklepios

NAME OF TOWN Translation Modern Name, If Any	LOCATION	DATE OF COIN
ΓΕΡΓΑ *Pergamum* Bergama	In ancient Mysia, now northwest Turkey	A.D. 180-192

Poppaea — Headdress of Isis

ΠΕΡΙΝΘΙΩΝ Perinthus	In ancient Thrace, now Turkey in Europe	A.D. 54-68

Man Restraining Bull — Horse

ΓΕΡΡΑΙΒΩΝ *Perrhaebi*	A tribe which occupied a section of Thessaly in Greece	480-400 B.C.

Geta — Pallas

ΠΕCCΙΝΟΥΝΤΙΩΝ *Pessinus*	In ancient Galatia, now eastern Turkey	A.D. 209-212

Ares — Nike

NAME OF TOWN		
Translation		
Modern Name, If Any	LOCATION	DATE OF COIN
ΓΕΤΗΛΙΝΩΝ	In the district of Bruttium in Italy	204-89 B.C.
Petelia		
Strongoli		

Herakles — Bull

ΦΑΙΣΤΙΩΝ   South coast of Crete   322-300 B.C.
Phaestus

Young Male Head — Horse

ΦΑΛΑΝΝΑΙΩΝ   In Thessaly, Greece   400-344 B.C.
Phalanna
Perrhaebia

Artemis Diktynna — Trident

ΦΑ   Northwest corner of Crete   330-270 B.C.
Phalasarna

Dionysus — Thyrsos

NAME OF TOWN
Translation
Modern Name, If Any

LOCATION

DATE OF COIN

ΦΑΝΑΓΟΡΙΤΩΝ
Phanagoria

In ancient Bosporus, now Russia

About 50 B.C.

Zeus — Eagle

ΦΑΡΝΑΚΕΩΝ
Pharnaceia

In northern Turkey, Black Sea
area. Formerly Pontus

1st Century B.C.

Zeus — Goat

ΦΑΡΙΩΝ
Pharos

An island in the Adriatic off
Yugoslavia, formerly Illyricum

4th century B.C.

Athena — Horse

ΦΑΡ
Pharsalus
Thessaliotis

In the district of Thessaly in
Greece

480-344 B.C.

Demeter — Bull

ΦΕΝΙΚΟΝ
Pheneus

In the central Grecian Peloponnesus,
formerly Arcadia

About 360 B.C.

Horse — Corn

NAME OF TOWN Translation Modern Name, If Any	LOCATION	DATE OF COIN
ΦΕΡΑΙΟΥΝ *Pherae* Pelasgiotis	In Thessaly, Greece	450-400 B.C.

Herakles — Tripod

ΦΙΛΙΓΓΩΝ
Philippi

In Macedonia, Greece

357-330 B.C.

Caracalla — Hermes

ΦΙΛΙΠΠΟΠΟΛΕΙΤΩΝ
Philippopolis

In Thrace, now Bulgaria

A.D. 211-217

Young Head — Dolphin, Mussel, Corn

ΦΙΕΣΤΕΛΙΑ
Phistelia

In the Campanian district of Italy

380-350 B.C.

Bull — Ivy Leaves and Grapes

NAME OF TOWN		
Translation		
Modern Name, If Any	LOCATION	DATE OF COIN
ΦΛΕΙΑΣΙΟΝ	In ancient Phliasia, now northeast	4th century B.C.
Phlius	corner of Grecian Peloponnesus	

Woman's Head — Incuse Squares

	Western Turkey, formerly Ionia	400-330 B.C.
ΦΩΚΑΕΩΝ		
Phokaia		

Bull's Head — Apollo

ΦΩΚΕΩΝ	On the Greek mainland at the	357-346 B.C.
Phokis	head of the Attic peninsula	

Zeus — Eagle

ΠΙΜΩΛΙΣΩΝ	In ancient Paphlagonia, now	About 100 B.C.
Pimolisa	northern Turkey near Black Sea	
Osmandjik(?)		

Antoninus Pius—Ceres

ΠΛΩΤΕΙΝΟΠΟΛΕΙΤΩΝ	In the Thracian district of Greece	A.D. 138-161
Plotinopolis		

Bull's Head — Spearhead

NAME OF TOWN Translation Modern Name, If Any	LOCATION	DATE OF COIN
ΠΟΛΥΡΗΝΙΟΝ Polyrhenium Palaeokastro Kissamou	At the western end of the island of Crete	330-280 B.C.

Young Man's Head

| Populonia | In the Etrurian district of Italy | About 400 B.C. |

Poseidon — Bull

| ΓΟΜΕΙΔ Poseidonia Pesto | In the Lucanian district of Italy | 470-400 B.C. |

Poseidon Hippias — Female Head

| ΓΟΤΕΙ Potidaea | On the Chalcidian peninsula in Macedonia, Greece | 500-429 B.C. |

Persephone — Bee

| ΓΡΑΙΣΙΩΝ Praesus | At the eastern end of the island of Crete | 400-148 B.C. |

Goddess — Poseidon

NAME OF TOWN Translation Modern Name, If Any	LOCATION	DATE OF COIN
ΓΡΙΑΝΣΙΕΩΝ *Priansus*	An inland town in Crete	430-200 B.C.

Trajan — Zeus

| ΠΡΟΥΣΑΕΩΝ *Prusa (ad Olympum)* Brusa | In ancient Bithynia, now north-central Turkey | A.D. 98-117 |

Domitian — Homonoia

| ΠΡΟΥΣΙΕΩΝ *Prusias ad Hypium* Uskub | In Bithynia, now north-central Turkey | A.D. 81-96 |

Tiberius — Dikaiosyne

| ΠΡΥΜΝΗCCΕΩΝ *Prymnessus* Seulun | In ancient Phrygia, now central Turkey | A.D. 14-37 |

Julia Domna — Ariel

NAME OF TOWN Translation Modern Name, If Any	LOCATION	DATE OF COIN
PABBAΘMΩBHNΩN Rabbath-Moba	In ancient Arabia. Now in Trans- Jordan(?)	A.D. 193-211

Marcus Aurelius and Commodus — Leto

PAΦIA *Raphia*	On the coast of Palestine which was once ancient Judaea	A.D. 180-192

Poseidon — Trident

PAYKION *Rhaucus*	On the north coast of Crete	430-300 B.C.

Apollo — Tripod

PHΓINΩN *Rhegium* Reggio	In the district of Bruttium in Italy	270-203 B.C.

Helios — Rose

NAME OF TOWN Translation Modern Name, If Any	LOCATION	DATE OF COIN

PO∆ION
Rhodes

A prominent city on the northern part of the island of Rhodes

400-333 B.C.

Athena — Herakles
In the district of Apulia in Italy

PYBAΣTEINΩN
Rubastini

About 300 B.C.

Claudius II —- The Dioscuri
In ancient Pisidia, now south-central Turkey

CAΓAΛACC∈ΩN
Sagalassus
Aghlasan

A.D. 268-270

Demos — Dionysos
In western Turkey, formerly Lydia

CAΛHNΩN
Sala

2nd century A.D.

Female Head — Shield
In the district of Attica in Greece

ΣAΛA
Salamis

350-318 B.C.

Apollo — Horse

NAME OF TOWN Translation Modern Name, If Any	LOCATION	DATE OF COIN
ΣΑΛΑΓΙΝΩΝ *Salapia* Salpi	In the district of Apulia in Italy	250-200 B.C.

Lion — Bull

| ΣΑΜΙ
Samos | An island off the west coast of Turkey. It had been a part of ancient Ionia | 408-394 B.C. |

Athena — Kybele

| ΣΑΜΟ
Samothrace | An island in the Aegean south of Thrace | About 280 B.C. |

Cista Mystica — Snakes

| ΣΑΡΔΙΑΝΩΝ
Sardes | The capital of ancient Lydia, now western Turkey | About 133 B.C. |

Forepart of Flying Horse — Palm Tree

| ΣΚΗΨΙΟΝ
Scepsis
Kourshounli-tepeh | In the ancient Troas, now north-western Turkey | 460-400 B.C. |

Young Head — Incuse Squares

NAME OF TOWN Translation Modern Name, If Any	LOCATION	DATE OF COIN
ΣΚΙΩΝΑΙΩΝ *Scione*	In Macedonia, Greece	About 400 B.C.

C∈BACTHNΩN
Sebaste

Domitian — City God
In ancient Samaria, now
Palestine

A.D. 81-96

C∈BACTOΠOΛITΩN
Sebastopolis-Heracleopolis
Sulu-Serai

Reverse, Temple
Northern Turkey at the Black Sea,
formerly called Pontus

A.D. 209-212

ΣΕΓΕΣΤΑΙΟΝ
Segesta
Sestri

Hound — Nymph
On the northwestern coast of
Sicily

480-461 B.C.

Gordianus III — Nike

NAME OF TOWN Translation Modern Name, If Any	LOCATION	DATE OF COIN
CEΛΕΥΚΕΩΝ *Seleuceia ad* *Calycadnum* Selefke	In ancient Cilicia, now southeastern Turkey	A.D. 238-244

Tyche — Thunderbolt

ΣΕΛΕΥΚΕΩΝ
Seleuceia Piera
Seleukiyeh

This was the port of Antioch in Syria

About 104 B.C.

Wrestlers — Slinger

ΣΕΛΓΕΩΝ
Selge
Seruk

In Pisidia, now south-central Turkey

3rd to 2nd century B.C.

Herakles and Bull — Hypsas

ΣΕΛΙΝΟΝΤΙΟΝ
Selinus

On the southwest coast of Sicily

466-415 B.C.

Caracalla — Hera

NAME OF TOWN Translation Modern Name, If Any	LOCATION	DATE OF COIN
CЄPΔIKHC *Serdica* Sofia	At one time in Thrace, now in Bulgaria	A.D. 211-217

Frog — Incuse Squares

ΣEPI
Seriphos(?)

An island in the Cyclades group
in the Aegean

About 540 B.C.

Naked Horseman — Incuse Squares

ΣEPMVΛIKON
Sermyle
Ormylia

In Macedon, Greece

About 500 B.C.

Zeus — Demeter(?)

ΣHΣAM
Sesamus

In ancient Paphlagonia, now
north-central Turkey

340-300 B.C.

Chimaera — Dove

NAME OF TOWN
Translation
Modern Name, If Any

LOCATION

DATE OF COIN

ΣΙ
Sicyon

In the district of Sicyon, north-western part of the Grecian Peloponnesus

About 350 B.C.

Athena — Apollo

ΣΙΔΗΤΩΝ
Side
Eski-Adalia

In south-central Turkey, formerly ancient Pamphylia

400-300 B.C.

Head of City Goddess — Eagle

ΣΙΔΩΝΙΩΝ
Sidon

In ancient Phoenicia, now Lebanon

1st century B.C.

Hermes — Seilenos and Boar

SEIC
Signia
Segni

In the district of Latium in Italy

300-280 B.C.

117

Gordian III and Tranquillina — Tyche

NAME OF TOWN Translation Modern Name, If Any	LOCATION	DATE OF COIN
CINΓAPA *Singara*	In ancient Mesopotamia, now Iraq	A.D. 238-244

Sinope — Eagle

ΣINΩ *Sinope* Sinub	A city in ancient Paphlagonia, now a part of north-central Turkey	322-220 B.C.

Apollo — Flying Eagle

Σlφ *Siphnos*	An island in the Cyclades group in the Aegean Sea	5th century B.C.

Apollo — Homer

ΣMYPNAIΩN Smyrna Izmir	In classical Ionia, now the west coast of Turkey	2nd century B.C.

Archer, Kneeling — Grapes

ΣOΛEΩN *Soli-Pompeiopolis*	In the southeast part of Turkey, formerly ancient Cilicia	450-386 B.C.

Zeus — Eagle

NAME OF TOWN Translation Modern Name, If Any	LOCATION	DATE OF COIN
ΣΤΡΑΤΟΝΙΚΕΩΝ *Stratoniceia* Eski-Hissar	In ancient Caria, now southwestern Turkey	166-88 B.C.

Herakles — Bird's Head

ΣΤΥΜΦΑΛΙΟΝ *Stymphalus*	In Arcadia on the central Peloponnesus, Greece	400-362 B.C.

Athena — Cock

ϟVEϟANO *Suessa Aurunca* Sessa	In the Campanian district of Italy	268-240 B.C.

Bull — Same Type, Incuse

ΣΥΒΑΡΙ *Sybaris*	This town (from which we have acquired our word sybarite) was in the Lucanian district of Italy	550-510 B.C.

Dionysus — Hermes

ΣΥΒΡΙΤΙΩΝ *Sybrita*	Formerly a town in the central part of Crete	400-300 B.C.

Caracalla — Apollo

NAME OF TOWN Translation Modern Name, If Any	LOCATION	DATE OF COIN
CY∈ΔP∈ ωΝ *Syedra* Sedra	In ancient Cilicia, now southeastern Turkey	A.D. 211-217

Arethusa — Quadriga

ΣΥΡΑΚΟΣΙΟΝ On the southeast coast of Sicily 317-310 B.C.
Syracuse
Siracusa

Augustus — Zeus

ΤΑΒΗΝΩΝ In ancient Caria, now western 29 B.C. - A.D. 14
Tabae Turkey
Davas

Boeotian Shield — Incuse Square

TANA In the Boeotian district of Greece 600-480 B.C.
Tanagra

Rider — Taras

ΤΑΡΑΣ In the district of Calabria in Italy 380-345 B.C.
Tarentum (Taras)
Taranto

Female Head — Ares

NAME OF TOWN		
Translation		
Modern Name, If Any	LOCATION	DATE OF COIN
ΤΕΡΣΙΚΟΝ	In ancient Cilicia, now southeastern	379-374 B.C.
Tarsus	Turkey	

Apollo — Tripod

TAYPOMENITAN
Tauromenium
Taormina

North of Mt. Etna on the north-eastern corner of Sicily

275-210 B.C.

Pallas — Owl

TIATI
Teate
Chieti

In the district of Apulia in Italy

About 300 B.C.

Gorgon — Three "E's" Back to Back

ΤΕΓΕΑΤΑΝ
Tegea

In Arcadia, central Peloponnesus

420-370 B.C.

Asklepios, Reverse

ΤΗΜΝΕΙΤΩΝ
Temnus

In ancient Aeolis, now north-western Turkey

A.D. 238-244

121

Janiform (Male and Female Heads) —
Double-Headed Axe

NAME OF TOWN
Translation
Modern Name, If Any

LOCATION

DATE OF COIN

TENEΔION
Tenedos

An island off the Troad, now off
the northwestern coast of Turkey

After 189 B.C.

Grapes — Incuse

TENIΩN
Tenos

An island off the Troad, now off
in the Aegean Sea

530-500 B.C.

Griffin — Incuse Square

THION
Teos

In ancient Ionia which is now
western Turkey

544-394 B.C.

Terina — Winged Nike

TEPINAION
Terina

In the district of Bruttium in Italy

About 360 B.C.

122

Hermes — Athena

NAME OF TOWN		
Translation		
Modern Name, If Any	LOCATION	DATE OF COIN

TEPMHCCΕΩN
Termessus Major

Was located in south-central Turkey, *formerly called Pisidia*

Struck during *the time of the* early Roman Empire

Satyr — Goat

TEPΩNAON
Terone

In Macedonia, Greece

424-420 B.C.

Dionysus — Herakles

ΘΑΣΙΟΝ
Thasos

An island off the coast of Thrace in the northern part of the Aegean Sea

After 146 B.C.

Demeter — Protesilaos

ΘΗΒΑΙΩΝ
Thebae
Phthiotis

In Thessaly, Greece

302-286 B.C.

Shield — Amphora

NAME OF TOWN Translation Modern Name, If Any	LOCATION	DATE OF COIN
ΘΗΒΑΙΩΝ *Thebes*	In the district of Boeotia in Greece	379-338 B.C.

Demeter — Horse

ΘΕΛ
Thelpusa — In Arcadia, central Grecian Peloponnesus — 400-370 B.C.

Man's Head — Bull

ΘΕΟΔΕΩ
Theodosia — In Russia on the Black Sea. This area formerly had been called the Tauric Chersonesus — 3rd century B.C.

Two Dolphins — Incuse Square

ΘΗΡ
Thera(?)
Santorin — In the Cyclades group of islands in the Aegean Sea — Around 550 B.C.

Shield — Aphrodite

ΘΕΣΓΙΚΟΝ
Thespiae — In the district of Boeotia in Greece — 387-374 B.C.

Athena — Bull

NAME OF TOWN Translation Modern Name, If Any	LOCATION	DATE OF COIN
ΘΟΥΡΙΩΝ Thurium	In the district of Lucania in Italy	425-400 B.C.

Plotina — Inscription

| ΘΥΑΤΕΙΡΗΝΩΝ
Thyatira
Ak-Hissar | In ancient Lydia, now western Turkey | A.D. 98-117 |

Pegasos — Athena

| ΘΥΡΡΕΙΩΝ
Thyrrheion | Was located in Acarnania which is now a part of the west coast of Greece opposite the island of Cephalonia | 350-250 B.C. |

Gordian III and Tranquillina — Tyche

| TOMEΩC
Tomis | In the district of the Danube River, now Romania | A.D. 238-244 |

Ear of Corn — Incuse Squares

| TΡΑΙΛΙΟΝ
Tragilus | In the Macedonian district of Greece | 450-400 B.C. |

Cista Mystica — Snakes Intertwined

NAME OF TOWN Translation Modern Name, If Any	LOCATION	DATE OF COIN
ΤΡΑΛΛΙΑΝΩΝ *Tralles*	Was located in Lydia, now a part of the west coast of Turkey	2nd century B.C.

Gordian III — Tyche

| ΤΡΑΠΕΖΟΥΝΤΙΩΝ
Trapezus
Trebizond | In ancient Pontus, now Turkey,
on the coast of the Black Sea | A.D. 238-244 |

Bull — Horse

| ΤΡΙΚΚΑΙΩΝ
Tricca
Histiaeotis | In Thessaly, Greece | 480-400 B.C. |

The Dioscuri — Tyche

| ΤΡΙΠΟΛΙΤΩΝ
Tripolis | In that part of ancient Phoenicia
which is now Syria | 142-81 B.C. |

Sleeping Dog — Lyre

NAME OF TOWN		
Translation		
Modern Name, If Any	LOCATION	DATE OF COIN
Tuder	In the district of Umbria in Italy	About 250 B.C.
Todi		

Hera — Apollo

ΤΥΛΙΣΙΩΝ   On the north coast of Crete   400-300 B.C.
Tylisus

Melkart-Herakles — Eagle

ΤΥΡΙΩΝ   In that part of ancient Phoenicia   126 B.C. - A.D. 57
Tyre   which is now encompassed by
Sur   Lebanon

Athena — Lion

ΥΕΛΗΤΩΝ   In the division of Lucania in Italy   About 350 B.C.
Velia (Hyele)

127

Athena — Owl

NAME OF TOWN		
Translation		
Modern Name, If Any	LOCATION	DATE OF COIN
VE	In the district of Apulia in Italy	Before 268 B.C.
Venusia		
Venosa		

Sun—Aphrodite

OYPANIΔΩN
Uranopolis

In Macedonia, Greece, on the
peninsula of Acte

About 300 B.C.

Apollo — Tripod

I AKYNΘOΣ
Zacynthus

An island off the coast of the
western Peloponnesus in Greece

370-350 B.C.

Centaur with Nymph — Incuse Squares

I AIEΛEΩN
Zaeelii

In Macedonia, Greece

Before 480 B.C.

PEOPLE AND DEVICES SEEN
ON GREEK COINS

Achelous

A Greek god who represented rivers. He is shown as having the body of a bull and the head of a man.

Agrippina the Younger

She was the mother of the Emperor Nero, sister of the Emperor Caligula, wife of the Emperor Claudius.

Aeneas

The son of Anchises in Homeric legend. Homer has it that Aeneas carried Anchises, too old to walk, from the desolated city of Troy after the Greeks had entered with their famous horse.

Ajax

A hero of Homer's "Iliad" known for his great strength.

Amphora

A vessel commonly used to hold wine.

Agrippa

One of Rome's great generals associated with the Emperor Augustus. He died in 12 B.C.

Antoninus Pius

Roman Emperor from A.D. 138-161. His was a peaceful and wise reign.

Aphrodite

The goddess of love. She was the Astarte of the Phoenicians, the Ishtar of the Babylonians, the Venus of the Romans.

Arethusa

She was a nymph who was changed into a river by the goddess Artemis, and made to flow under the sea until rising again in a fountain on the island of Ortygia.

Apollo

One of the most revered of the Greek gods. Among other things he represented music, poetry, manliness and was also keeper of the herds. As a matter of fact, there were few attributes he did not possess.

Artemis

This was a sister of Apollo. She was goddess of the hunt, of wild things in nature, of rivers and of lakes. The Greeks even bestowed upon her the paradoxical attribute of being the goddess of virginity and of childbirth. To the Romans she was known as Diana.

Ares

A son of Zeus and Hera, he was god of war. Later the Romans would call him Mars.

Asklepios

This was the god of healing and of medicine. Homer said he was a physician. He raised his ability to such an extent that he was able to bring the dead back to life.

This was too much for the father of the gods, Zeus, who slew him.

Augustus

The first Emperor of Rome. He ruled from 29 B.C. to A.D. 14.

Astarte

The Phoenician name for the goddess, Aphrodite.

Bellona

A war-like goddess.

Athena

One of the most prominent of all the Greek deities, Athena represented many things. She was the city goddess of Athens and of Corinth. She was goddess of peace and of war. As Hygeia she represented the health of the nation; as Hippia she was the tamer of horses. When she appears with wings she is Nike...victory. She was born by the questionable process of springing from the head of her father, Zeus.

Belos

A river god, one of many invented by the Greeks. This merely emphasizes the importance of water to humanity.

131

Biga

A chariot drawn by two horses.

Caracalla

Roman Emperor, A.D. 211-217.

Caduceus

A staff about which are entwined two serpents. To the ancients it represented the staff of Hermes. To moderns it is the symbol of the medical profession.

Centaur

A half man, half horse personifying a mythical race of people who lived in Thessaly.

Caligula

Debauched and insane Emperor of the Romans from A.D. 37-41.

Chimaera

A monster (female) who spit flames, had the head of a lion, the body of a goat and the tail of a serpent.

Claudius II

Roman Emperor from A.D. 268-270.

Demos

A representation of democracy.

Dionysius

A major god of the Greeks who watched over the grapes. The wine made from the grapes was cause of revelry and licentiousness. In one of his milder forms he was god of the drama. The Romans would know him as Bacchus.

Commodus

The inept and cruel son of the Emperor Marcus Aurelius. He was Emperor from A.D. 180-192.

Demeter

Goddess of grain and agriculture.

Dioscuri

These were the twins, Castor and Pollux, sons of Leda and Zeus.

Domitia

The wife of the Emperor Domitian. She was one of a group who fatally poisoned her husband.

Faustina the Younger

Wife of the Emperor Marcus Aurelius. She died in A.D. 175.

Domitian

Roman Emperor from A.D. 81-96.

Fulmen

The thunderbolt, symbol of Zeus.

Elagabalus

Roman Emperor from A.D. 218-222 .

Gallienus

Roman Emperor from A.D. 253-268 .

Europa

A personification of Europe.

Geta

Roman Emperor from A.D. 209-212.

Gordian III and Tranquillina

Roman Emperor from A.D. 238-244, and his wife.

Hadrian

Emperor of Rome from A.D. 117-138.

Gorgon

The name comes from the Greek meaning "terrible." One glance at a coin bearing the gorgon's image will serve to emphasize this appellation. At one time the Greeks had Medusa represented as the gorgon. Then, one looking upon her would be turned to stone. It can be assumed that the myth has been buried with the ages.

Helios

The Greek sun-god.

Hephaestos

The Greek god of fire. The Romans, later, would call him Vulcan. He was afflicted with a lame leg incurred by having been thrown out of heaven by Zeus for siding with his mother, Hera, in an argument with Zeus.

Griffin

A mythological monster, half lion, half eagle. In the lore of the ancient Scythians (Scythia is now a part of Russia) this horrible creature guarded their gold.

Hera

Sister and wife of Zeus, Hera ruled over the heavens with him. As was true with many other deities she represented many things to the Greeks, among which were patron of the widowed and goddess of the earth and moon.

Herennius Etruscus

Son of the Roman Emperor Trajan Decius, he was slain with his father while battling the Goths in Thrace. (A.D. 251).

Hercules (or Herakles)

A son of Zeus and the symbol of strength.

Homer

The great creator of the "Iliad" and the "Odyssey."

Hermes

Another son of Zeus, he was the messenger and herald of the gods. Not satisfied with such minimal activities, the Greeks had him representing cunning, trickery, science, theft, invention, eloquence, and as the companion of those being transported to Hades.

Hygeia (With Asklepios)

The daughter of Asklepios and the personification of health.

Incuse

This word comes from the Latin infinitive "incudere," to forge (with a hammer). Thus, coins with incuse reverses show the punch marks where they have been struck.

Kanthoros

A deep cup.

Kithara

An ancient Greek lyre.

Janiform

In the form of Janus, thus, appearing like Janus, the Roman god with two heads facing in opposite directions symbolical of many things, one of which was that he could look into the past and the future at the same time.

Kybele

To the people of Anatolia she was the goddess of the earth. She was the founder and protector of cities, the mother of mankind, etc.

Julia Domna

Livia

The wife of the emperor Augustus.

Maenad

A helper to Dionysius in his orgiastic rites.

Lucius Verus

Co-ruler with Marcus Aurelius. He died in A.D. 169 at the age of 39.

Marcus Aurelius

Roman Emperor A.D. 161-180.

Lulav

The palm branch which is used in the Jewish ritual of the Feast of the Tabernacle.

Melqarth-Herakles

Hercules represented as Melqarth, patron of the Phoenician city of Tyre.

Macrinus

Roman Emperor, A.D. 217-218.

Nero

Roman Emperor, A.D. 54-68.

Nerva

Roman Emperor, A.D. 96-98.

Nike

The goddess of Victory, oft-times called the Winged Victory. A famous and magnificent representation of her is in the Louvre museum in Paris.

Otacilia Severa

Wife of the emperor Philip I of Rome.

Pallas

One of the names by which the goddess Athena was called. Pallas was the name of a giant slain by her.

Pegasos

The winged horse of the muses. He carried their hopes, their inspirations and their poetry into the skies.

Plotina

The wife of the Roman Emperor Trajan.

Poppaea

One of the wives of the Emperor Nero.

Protesilaos

The first Greek killed at Troy. Legend has it that the first Greek to set foot upon land after the long voyage to Troy, would die. He volunteered.

Septimius Severus

Roman Emperor, A.D. 193-211.

Quadriga

A chariot or cart drawn by four horses.

Serapis

A god prominent in Egypt under the Ptolemies, and then throughout the Greek world. He was god of sun, life and fruitfulness.

Sabina

The wife of the Emperor Hadrian. She died in A.D. 137.

Silenos

The father of Bacchus.

Severus Alexander

Roman Emperor, A.D. 222-235.

Silphium

A now extinct plant used by the Greeks for medicinal purpose.

Sybil

A sybil (or sibyl) is a prophetess.

Sphinx

The ancient Greek sphinx, not to be confused with the Egyptian variety, was known throughout the Greek world. The most famous was at Thebes in Boeotia, had the body of a lion, wings and the head of a woman. The sphinx posed a riddle to all who passed and those failing to answer correctly were destroyed.

Syrinx

Pan pursued this nymph and turned her into a reed which he used to play his pipes.

Taras

The founder of the city of Tarentum in Italy. He was rescued from a shipwreck by a dolphin upon which he rode safely to shore. The city was founded where they touched land. It is the present-day Taranto.

Thyrsos

A staff surrounded by grapes, the symbol of Bacchus.

Tiberius

Emperor of Rome during the time of Christ. His rule extended from A.D. 14-37.

Trajan

Roman Emperor during its greatest extent, A.D. 98-117.

Tyche

The Greek goddess of fortune.

Triptolemos

He was said to have given grain and the knowledge of its cultivation to mankind. Often he used a chariot in which he drove about the Greek world.

Zeus

The greatest of the Greek gods, father of all. Romans later called him Jupiter. He was worshipped under innumerable titles, Zeus Soter (Savior); Olympus (seated on Mt. Olympus, crown of the Greek world and home of the gods); Philios (hospitality); Basileus (king); Hades (the underworld); Panhellenios (of all the Greeks); and many others. He was a vigorous and unrepenting bigamist having been married to such beauties as Hera, Demeter, Semele, Maia, Alcmene, Mnemosyne, Eurynome and, more than likely, others.

Triskeles

A three-branched figure possessing a common figure, usually in the form of legs. The word itself means "three-legged."

THE GREEK KINGS, SATRAPS
AND TYRANTS

While some of the Greek kings in one way or another altered the stream of history, many of them are scarcely remembered today. Their inclusion in this book, therefore, serves the purpose of giving the reader an opportunity to study some of the interesting coins which were issued by these people. As these pages are turned, many coins will appear, some of which are the distillation of the finest in Greek portraiture. Upon one there is the suggestion of a smile, upon another the features are set hard, a manifestation, almost, of cruelty. One has his eyes turned to the heavens as if in some mute appeal to a higher King. And again, it would appear that some engraver approached his task with distaste and portrayed his ruler as a sensuous, full jowled and weak individual, evidences of the excesses which his power had stamped upon his countenance. And so there is a certain delight to these coins, if not too much historical value. It should be remembered that many of these kings ruled only because of the sufferance of others more powerful and that they had little to command other than by supervision. In many instances, their master, Rome, informed them how to conduct their affairs and the Imperial legions were at hand as a reminder.

The reader will note the similarity of the portraits of many of the kings of the same lineage, particularly among the Ptolemies of Egypt. Compare a coin of Alexander the Great with these Egyptian coins and this similarity is at once noticeable. The Ptolemies were the successors to Alexander and his power had been of such an extent as to preclude, for some time, anyone altering his image upon the coins. And so, in many instances, the portrait is not of the ruling Ptolemy, but of Alexander.

Those who ruled the ancient countries and were identified by portraits and inscriptions on these coins were known by many titles. Most prevalent were the Kings and Emperors. Others were called Satraps. The term was applied to the governor of a province under the Persian monarchy. In ancient Rome the ruler of a province was called a Procurator.

In ancient Greece the title of Tyrant was used by a king or ruler who held absolute power over his subjects. This term did not originally indicate an abuse of such authority, but has come to signify a ruler of undue severity or harshness. A Usurper was one who wrongfully seized power by force of strength and occupied the throne without right.

Throughout the ancient world the right to hold power and title was often passed on through a family or by appointment of the ruling monarch. In the late Roman empire it was not uncommon for an aspiring emperor to bid money for support in an election.

AGRIGENTUM
(A famous city on the south coast of Sicily, now called Agrigento.)

Phintias—A tyrant who developed complete control over this community and other communities in Sicily as well. He ruled from 287-279 B.C.

ARMENIA
(In Russia and in Turkey.)

Arsames—A ruler of Armenia about 230 B.C.

Abdissares—Ruled in Armenia about 200 B.C.

Xerxes — A ruler of Sophene (the western part of Armenia) about 170 B.C.

Zariadres—A ruler of that portion of western Armenia known as Sophene.

Morphilig—Ruled between 150-148 B.C.

Tigranes—King of Armenia between 97-56 B.C. The Syrians called him to quell the serious fighting in their country and he was successful in doing so.

Artavasdes II—The son of Tigranes I. He ruled from 56-31 B.C.

Tigranes III—The son of Artavasdes. His reign lasted twelve years, from 20-8 B.C.

Tigranes IV—Ruled from 8-5 B.C.

Artavasdes III—The son of Ariobarzanes II who was king of Media Atropatene (in ancient Persia, now Iran). He ruled from 5-2 B.C.

Artaxias—A son of Polemo I, king of Pontus (a country which lay along the south shore of the Black Sea, now a part of Turkey). His reign was from A.D. 18-35.

BACTRIA
(A country now a part of moderan Iran.)

Diodotos—A king of Bactria, 256-239 B.C. Not too much is known of him.

Euthydemos I—Ruled from 230-190 B.C.

Euthydemos II—Son of Demetrios. 190-171 B.C.

Pantaleon—A probable successor of Euthydemos II. Little is known of him.

Demetrios—Son of Euthydemos I. He enlarged his territory, spreading into India. 205-171 B.C.

Agathokles—Ruled with Pantaleon and might have been his successor.

Antimachus—A contemporary of Agathokles.

Theophilus—Apparently a Bactrian ruler, but his date of rule is obscure.

Lysias—His reign was about 145-135 B.C.

Diomedes—Date of rule uncertain.

Archebius—Date of rule uncertain.

Eucratides—Eucratides was king of Bactria and India. His reign was from about 171-135 B.C.

Apollodotos—Ruled from 156-140 B.C.

Agathocleia—The mother of Strato I. She ruled during his minority.

Heliokles—The son of Eucratides. He ruled from about 135-110 B.C.

Antialkidas—A Bactrian ruler from about 145-135 B.C.

Strato I—Probably a contemporary of Heliokles (130-110 B.C.)

Menander—One of the better known of the Bactrian kings who ruled from 160-140 B.C.

Epander—Date of rule around 135-130 B.C.

Dionysios—Date of rule around 80-75 B.C.

Zoilos—Ruled about 150-145 B.C.

Apollophanes—Date of rule uncertain.

Artemidorus—Date of rule uncertain.

Hippostratos—About 80-60 B.C.

Amyntas—Date of rule about 60-40 B.C.

Peukolaus—Date of rule around 80-60 B.C.

Polyxenos—Date of rule about 135-130 B.C.

Telephos—Date of rule around 80-75 B.C.

INDO-SCYTHIAN

Antimachus II—Date of rule uncertain.

Philoxenus—About 125 B.C.

Nicias—Date of rule uncertain.

Azes—Ruled about 57-35 B.C.

Azilises—Ruled about 57-35 B.C.

Hermaios—Ruled from about 40-1 B.C.

BITHYNIA
(A country formerly along the southwest coast of the Black Sea. Now a part of Turkey.)

Timotheus—A tyrant of Heracleia Pontica in Bithynia. The probable dates of his rule were 345-337 B.C.

Dionysius—Ruled with Timotheus from 345-337 B.C. and then by himself from 337-305 B.C.

Zipoetes I—Ruled probably from 298-279 B.C. He struck no coins.

Nikomedes I—Son of Zipoetes I. Ruled probably from 279-255 B.C.

Ziaelas—Son of Nikomedes I. Ruled from 255-228 B.C.

Prusias I—Son of Ziaelas. His rule extended from about 228-185 B.C.

Prusias II—Son of Prusias I.

Approximate dates of his rule were from 185-149 B.C.

Nikomedes IV—94-74 B.C. were the approximate dates of his rule.

Nikomedes II—Son of Prusias II. His rule extended from 149-128 B.C. approximately.

CAPPADOCIA
(A country which occupied what is now part of eastern Turkey.)

Ariarathes I—Ruled from 330-322 B.C.

Ariarathes II—Son of the first Ariarathes. The probable dates of his rule are 301-280 B.C.

Ariaramnes—The son of Ariarathes II. His reign had the probable dates of 280-230 B.C.

Ariarathes III—The son of Ariarammes. Ruled from about 250-220 B.C.

Nikomedes III—Son of the second Nikomedes. Probably ruled from 128-94 B.C.

Ariarathes IV—Son of Ariarathes III. His rule dates from 220-163 B.C.

Ariarathes V—Son of the above. Ruled from 163-130 B.C.

Orophernes—A pretender to the throne. Ruled from 158-157 B.C.

Ariarathes VI—He ruled, probably, from 130-116 B.C. Son of Ariarathes V.

Ariarathes VII—Son of the above. The approximate dates of his rule are 116-101 B.C.

Ariarathes VIII—Another son of Ariarathes VI. Ruled from 101-100 B.C. and appears to have struck very few coins.

Ariarathes IX—Son of Mith-

radates VI, king of Pontus. He ruled from 101-87 B.C.

Ariobarzanes I—His reign extended from 95-63 B.C.

Ariobarzanes II—Son of the above. Ruled from 63-52 B.C.

Ariobarzanes III—Ruled from 52-42 B.C. He was the son of Ariobarzanes II.

Ariarathes X—This was a brother of Ariobarzanes III. He ruled from 42-36 B.C.

Archelaus—When Cappadocia became a Roman province at his death, he had ruled for 53 years. (36 B.C.-A.D.17)

CARIA
(A country which occupied that region which is now the southwest part of Turkey.)

Hekatomnus—A satrap of Caria who ruled from 395-377 B.C.

Maussollos—Also a satrap of Caria. His name has been left to posterity because of the monument erected in his memory by his wife. To this day we call such an edifice a mausoleum. He ruled from 377-353 B.C.

Hidrieus—A son of Hecatomnus who married his own sister. He ruled from 351-344 B.C.

Pixodaros—Another son of Hecatomnus. He ruled from 340-344 B.C.

Rhoontopates—As satrap, he ruled from 334-333 B.C. and attempted to defend Halicarnassus against Alexander the Great.

CILICIA
(A country, now a part of Turkey, which occupied, roughly, an area on the southeast coast of the Mediterranean above Syria.)

Tiribazus—A ruler of Tarsus, in Cilicia. His reign covered six years from 386-380 B.C.

Pharnabazos—Also a ruler of Tarsos in Cilicia. He ruled from 379-374 B.C.

Mazaios—This satrap ruled Cilicia from 361-334 B.C.

COMMAGENE
(An ancient country originally in the vicinity of northern Syria and eastern Cilicia and south of Cappadocia. Present day Turkey and Syria incorporate this area within their borders.)

Samos—A king of this area between the probable dates of 140-130 B.C.

Mithradates I—The son of Samos. He ruled about 96 B.C.

Mithradates II—Son of the above. Ruled probably about 92 B.C.

Antiochus I—Another son of Mithradates I who ruled from about 69-31 B.C.

Antiochus IV—His rule extended from A.D. 38-72.

Iotape—The wife of Antiochus IV.

Epiphanes and Callinicus—These two were sons of Antiochus IV and Iotape. Their reign started, probably, about A.D. 72.

CYPRUS

(An island at the far eastern end of the Mediterranean Sea. These kings ruled, generally, over city-communities rather than over the entire island.)

Euagoras I—A king of the city of Amathus, about 391 B.C.

Rhoecus—Conjecturally ruled at Amathus around 350 B.C.

Baalmelek I—A king of Citium who ruled from about 479-449 B.C.

Azbaal—Another king of Citium who ruled from 449-425 B.C. Citium is the present day Larnaka on the east coast of Cyprus.

Baalmelek II—King of Citium from about 425-400 B.C.

Baalram—Ruled Citium from about 400-392 B.C.

Melekiathon—His rule over Citium extended from 392-361 B.C.

Demonicus—Whether he ruled or not is uncertain. The dates of 388-387 are associated with him.

Pumiathon—Struck only gold coins. Reigned from 361-312 B.C. at Citium.

Gras—A ruler of Idalium on Cyprus about 460 B.C.

Stasikypros—Another ruler of Idalium from about 460-450 B.C.

Sidqimelek—A king of the city of Lapethus about 450 B.C.

Praxippus—Exact date of rule of Lapethus uncertain although he was deposed by Ptolemy about 312 B.C.

Stasioecus I and Timocharis—These two ruled over Marium, present day Chrysochou, some time during the latter half of the 5th century B.C.

Stasioechus II—A king of Marium deposed about 312 B.C.

Stasandros—Ruled over Paphos on the west coast of Cyprus about 450 B.C.

Timocharos—Ruled over Paphos about 385 B.C.

Timarchos—Another ruler of Paphos about 323 B.C.

Nikokles—The dates of his rule are uncertain although he probably died in 309 B.C.

Euanthes—A king of the city of Salamis, one of the most famous cities of Cyprus. He ruled about 450 B.C.

Abdemon—A ruler of Salamis before 411 B.C.

Euagoras I—Ruled Salamis from 411-373 B.C.

Nikokles II—His rule over Salamis extended from 373-361 B.C.

Euagoras II—Ruler of Salamis between 361-351 B.C.

Nikokreon—Ruled, probably, between 331-310 B.C.

Menelaus—He ruled from 310-306 B.C.

Pasikrates—A king of Soli, modern Karavostasi, whose rule encompassed the year 331 B.C.

Eunostos—The date of his rule is around 310 B.C.

EGYPT
(Egypt, when Alexander the Great's empire was divided at his death, came under the rule of one of his generals, Ptolemy.)

Ptolemy I—Called SOTER

(Preserver) he ruled Egypt from
305-283 B.C.

Ptolemy II—Called PHILADEL-
PHUS, he was the son of the 1st
Ptolemy and ruled from 285-246
B.C.

Ptolemy III—Called EUER-
GETES (Benefactor) his rule
extended from 246-221 B.C.

Ptolemy IV—He was called
PHILOPATOR (Loving his
father) ruling from 221-204 B.C.

Ptolemy V—His appellation was
EPIPHANES (Illustrious) and he
ruled from 204-180 B.C. He was
a child when he took the throne
and suffered the loss of much of
his territory.

Ptolemy VI—Was called PHILO-
METOR (Loving his mother).
Because of his youth the country
was ruled in his behalf by his
mother, Cleopatra. (Not the
famous Cleopatra.) His reign
extended from 180-145 B.C.

Ptolemy VII—He was murdered almost immediately after coming to the throne in the year 145 B.C. He was known as EUPATOR.

after the death of Ptolemy X. His second reign extended from 88-80 B.C.

Cleopatra III—Wife of Ptolemy X, this coin was struck sometime between 106-101 B.C.

Ptolemy VIII—Succeeded his nephew, Ptolemy VII in 145 B.C. and ruled until 116 B.C. He had the surname, PHYSCON (Fat Paunch), and was known as EUERGETES II.

Ptolemy IX—Succeeded his father and ruled from 116-106 B.C., leaving the throne to his brother Ptolemy X.

Ptolemy X—Known, also as ALEXANDER I, his rule extended from approximately 106-88 B.C.

Ptolemy XI—Also called ALEXANDER II, he ruled for only 19 days in the year 80 B.C. and issued no coins.

Ptolemy IX—Returned as ruler

Ptolemy XII—Was called NEOS DIONYSOS (the NEW Dionysos), and was surnamed, AULETES. He was the son of PTOLEMY XI. Ruled from 80-58 B.C. and then from 55-51 B.C.

Alexander—A king of Epirus from 342-326 B.C.

Pyrrhus—He ruled from 295-272 B.C.

Cleopatra VII—This is the famous Cleopatra, daughter of Auletes and lover of Marc Antony. She controlled her brothers, Ptolemy XIV, Ptolemy XV, and Ptolemy XVI, who was her son. She ruled from 51-30 B.C.

GALATIA
(A country which extended across what is now central Turkey.)

Deiotarus I—Deiotarus ruled between the approximate dates of 64-40 B.C.

Brogitarus—Ruled about 58 B.C.

Ptolemy XIV—A brother to Cleopatra and ruling only through her.

Ptolemy XV—Another brother to Cleopatra.

Ptolemy XVI—The son of Cleopatra, known as CAESARI-ON. His rule was determined by Cleopatra's actions.

Amyntas—His rule encompassed the years from 36-25 B.C.

EPIRUS
(A country which is now incorporated into western Greece and Albania.)

HERACLEIA PONTICA
(A part of ancient Bithynia which now lies within Turkey, along the Black Sea.)

Satyrus—A tryant who ruled from 352-345 B.C.

Timotheus and Dionysius—The rule of these two tyrants extended from 345-337 B.C.

Clearchus and Oxathres—These tryants ruled from 305-302 B.C.

ILLYRIA
(A country which is now included in Yugoslavia and Albania, along the Adriatic coast.)

Monunios—Ruled about 300 B.C.

Genthios—Probably ruled between 197-168 B.C.

Ballaios—Little is known of this ruler. He probably ruled from 167-135 B.C.

THE KINGS AND PRINCES OF JUDAEA
(Judaea lay in the Dead Sea area of what is now Palestine.)

THE ASMONAEAN
(Or Hasmonean) PRINCES

(These princes were of the

family of the Maccabees probably deriving their name from an earlier ancestor.)

Simon Maccabaeus—Ruled from 143-135 B.C.

John Hyrcanus I—His rule extended from 135-105 B.C.

Judas Aristobulus—Reigned from 104-103 B.C.

Alexander Jannaeus—Ruled from 103-76 B.C.

Alexandra Salome—The widow of Jannaeus (76-67 B.C.)

John Hyrcanus II—Apparently ruled intermittently between 67-40 B.C.

Alexander II—65-49 B.C.

Antigonos—Ruled from 40-37 B.C. He was also known as Mattathias.

THE IDUMAEAN PRINCES OF JUDAEA
(These princes probably inherited their common appellation because their line came from

ancient Idumaea, southeast of Palestine.)

Herod the Great—His rule extended from 40 B.C.-A.D. 4.

Herod Archelaus—Archelaus reigned from 4 B.C. to A.D. 6.

Herod Antipas—Ruled over Galilaea from 4 B.C. to A.D. 39.

Herod Philip II—Ruled Batanaea, Trachonitis, and Hauranitis in Judaea from 4 B.C. to A.D. 34.

Herod Agrippa I—His reign coincided with that of the emperor Caligula. (A.D. 37-44.)

Herod—A brother of Agrippa I. He was king of Chalcis.

Agrippa II—Ruled from A.D. 56-95.

Aristobulus—Son of Herod, king of Chalis.

MACEDONIA
(The northern part of Greece, Macedon is best known as having been the birthplace of Alexander the Great. Macedon was ruled by kings beginning in 498 B.C.)

Alexander I—This man ruled 44 years in all, from 498-454 B.C.

Perdiccas II—His reign was from 454-413 B.C.

Archelaus I—Son of Perdicas II, his rule was from 413-399 B.C.

Archelaus II—396-392 B.C.

Amyntas II—Ruled for a short time, between 392-390 B.C.

Pausanias—This reign, too, was short (390-389 B.C.)

Amyntas III—Amyntas ruled twice and with the exception of the year 382 B.C., his reign extended from 389-369 B.C.

Alexander II—Ruled from 369-368 B.C. He probably struck no coins.

Perdiccas III—Ruled from about 365-359 B.C.

Philip II—Father of Alexander the Great and a famous ruler in his own right. His reign extended from 359-336 B.C.

Alexander the Great—King of Macedonia and most of the known world from 336-323 B.C. His conquests are all the more remarkable when it is considered that he died when he was 33 years of age. That he loved power there is little doubt, but he was well educated, the great philosopher Aristotle having been one of his teachers. It can be said that he brought Greek culture into the East.

Philip III—Known as Aridaeus, he ruled from 323-316 B.C.

Cassander—His name appears upon certain bronze coins. He ruled from 316-297 B.C.

Philip IV—Son of Cassander, ruled from 297-296 B.C.

Alexander V—Another son of Cassander. Ruled during the year 295 B.C. It is not known whether he struck coins.

Antigonus—Was known as "King of Asia." Ruled from 306-301 B.C. He was the father of Demetrius Poliorcetes.

Antigonus Gonatas and Antigonus Doson—There is a question of the coinage of these two rulers and to whom it belongs. Gonatas ruled from 277-239 B.C., and Doson from 229-220 B.C.

Demetrius II—Ruled from 239-229 B.C.

Demetrius Poliorcetes—Demetrius, "the besieger," for that is what "poliorcetes" means, ruled from 306-283 B.C.

Pyrrhus—Ruled, interruptedly, from 287-272 B.C.

Philip V—His rule was from 220-179 B.C.

Perseus—Ruled from 178-168 B.C.

MAURETANIA
(An ancient country which occupied what is now a part of Morocco and Algeria.)

Syphax—The dates of his rule are probably 213-202 B.C.

Vermina—The son of the above. Ruled around 200 B.C.

Bocchus—First half of 1st century B.C.

Bogud—Bogud was a king of western Mauretania from about 49-31 B.C.

Bocchus II—King of eastern Mauretania from about 49-38 B.C.

Juba II—One of the better-known kings of Mauretania, he was the husband of Selene, (daughter of Cleopatra and Marc Antony) and had been appointed to his throne by the emperor Augustus. He ruled from 25 B.C. to A.D. 23.

Ptolemy—Ruled from A.D. 23-40. He was the son of Juba 1.

THE KINGS OF NABATHAEA
(Nabathaea was an ancient country east and southeast of Palestine, probably in present day Trans Jordan.)

Aretas III—His rule extended from 87-62 B.C.

Obodas II—Son of Aretas III. Ruled from about 62-47 B.C.

Malichus I—Son of Obodas II. His rule lasted from 47-30 B.C.

Obodas III—Son of Malichus I and ruled from 30-9 B.C.

Aretas IV—A brother of Obodas III. He ruled from 9 B.C. to A.D. 40.

Malichus II—Son of Aretas IV. His reign was from A.D. 40-75.

Rabbel II—Son of Malichus II.

THE KINGS OF NUMIDIA
(Numidia was another North African country to the east of

Mauretania and now incorporated in Tunisia and Algeria.)

Masinissa—His rule extended from 202-148 B.C.

Micipsa—Probably ruled with his brothers from about 148-118 B.C.

Gulussa—Ruled from about 148-140 B.C.

Adherbal—118-112 B.C.

Jugurtha—His reign extended from 118-106 B.C.

Hiempsal II—Ruled from 106-60 B.C.

Mastanesosus—Ruled as dynast about 62 B.C.

Juba I—His rule carried from 60-46 B.C.

THE KINGS OF PARTHIA

(Parthia was an ancient country which, today, would be a part of modern Iran. Its kings were known as Arsacidae after the first member of the line, Arsakes.)

Arsakes—Ruled from about 238-211 B.C.

Tiridates I—Held the throne on two occasions. First from 248-247 B.C., then from 211-210 B.C.

Arsakes II—A son of Tiridates I, who ruled from 211-191 B.C.

Phriapatios—His reign was from 191-176 B.C.

Phraates I—The probable dates of Phraates' rule were 176-171 B.C.

Mithradates I—Ruled, probably, from 171-138 B.C.

Phraates II—His reign covered the years 138-127 B.C.

Artabanos II—His rule covered the years 88-77 B.C.

Sinatruces—77-70 B.C.

Phraates III—Reigned from 70-57 B.C.

Mithradates III—Ruled from 57-54 B.C.

Artabanos I—127-123 B.C.

Himerus ?—Possibly ruled from 124-123 B.C.

Orodes II—The dates of his rule probably extended from 57-38 B.C.

Pakoros—Was in power about 39 B.C.

Mithradates II—Reigned for 35 years, from 123-88 B.C.

Phraates IV—38-2 B.C.

Tiridates II—Possibly ruled in 26 B.C.

Artabanos III—Reigned for about 30 years, from A.D. 10 or 11 to 40.

Phraataces and Musa—Ruled from about 3 B.C. to A.D. 4. Musa was his mother.

Vardanes I—His rule carried through the years A.D. 41-45.

Gotarzes—Ruled from about A.D. 40 to 51.

Vonones I—Ruled from about the year A.D. 8-12.

Vonones II—This king issued no coins. He occupied the throne apparently during the year A.D. 51.

Volagases I—A.D. 51-77.

Vardanes II—The possessor of a short reign during the year A.D. 55.

Pakoros II—Apparently ruled from about A.D. 77 to 110.

Artabanos IV—Ruled from A.D. 80-81.

Osroes—The dates of his reign are

not definite, but would fall somewhere between A.D. 106-130.

Volagases II—Ruled for an extraordinary length of time, possibly 70 years, from A.D. 77-147.

Mithradates IV—About A.D. 130-147.

Volagases III—He was upon the throne from about A.D. 147-191.

Volagases IV—Ruled from A.D. 191 to about 207.

Volagases V—From A.D. 207 or 208 to 221 or 222.

Artabanos V—He ruled about A.D. 213-227.

whom Lysimachus entrusted to guard his fortune. He assumed authority in 282 B.C. and ruled until 263 B.C.

Artavasdes—Ruled from about A.D. 227-228.

THE KINGS OF PAPHLAGONIA
(Paphlagonia was an ancient country, the area of which would now be incorporated in north central Turkey.)

Pylaemenes—Ruled about 133 B.C.

Deiotarus—He ruled from 31-5 B.C.

Eumenes I—Ruled from 263-241 B.C. He was Philetairos' nephew.

THE KINGS OF PERGAMUM IN MYSIA
(Mysia was a country which would now be incorporated in northwestern Turkey and its principal city was Pergamum.)

Attalos I—His rule extended from 241-197 B.C.

Philetairos—This was the guard

166

Eumenes II—This was a son of Attalos who ruled from 197-160 B.C.

Attalos II—A brother of Eumenes II. He ruled from 159-138 B.C.

Attalos III—Reigned from 138-133 B.C.

THE KINGS OF PONTUS AND BOSPORUS
(Pontus occupied an area in the north central part of what is now Turkey, along the coast of the Black Sea. Bosporus was located in the vicinity of the Crimea on the Black Sea, now in Russia.)

Paerisades—The names of four obscure kings who ruled from about 280-100 B.C.

Spartocus—Ruled sometime during the 2nd century B.C.

Leucon II or III—Ruled sometime during the 2nd century B.C.

Pharnakes I—63-47 B.C.

Asander—His rule was from about 47 to 16 B.C.

Hygiaenon—First century B.C.

Akas—2nd century B.C.

Mithradates I—Ruler of Pontus from 302-265 B.C. He issued no coins.

Ariobarzanes—The son of Mithradates I of Pontus. He, too, issued no coins. Ruled, probably, from 265-255 B.C.

Mithradates II—His reign was approximately from 255-220 B.C.

Mithradates III—Son of Mithradates II. Probably ruled from 220-185 B.C.

Pharnakes II—Ruled from about 185-159 B.C.

Mithradates IV—159-150 B.C.

Mithradates V—His reign was from about 150-120 B.C.

Mithradates VI—This was the son

of Mithradates V. He was king of both Pontus and Bosporus from about 120 B.C. to 63 B.C.

Polemo I—Polemo was king of Pontus about 36 B.C.

Pythadoris—Pythadoris was the daughter of Polemo I and queen of Pontus from about 8 B.C. to A.D. 22.

Antonia Tryphaena—Antonia was the daughter of Polemo I, ruling from A.D. 22-49.

Polemo II—The son of Antonia Tryphaena. He was king of Pontus from about A.D. 38-65, and king of Bosporus from about A.D. 38-41.

THE LATER RULERS OF BOSPORUS

Aspurgus—From about 8 B.C. to A.D. 38.

Rhescuporis I—He ruled from A.D. 14-42.

Mithradates—A.D. 42-46.

Cotys I—Reigned from A.D. 46-78.

Rhescuporis II—A.D. 78-93.

Sauromates I—He ruled from about A.D. 93-124.

Cotys II—Ruled from about A.D. 124-132.

Rhoemetalces—He occupied the throne from about A.D. 131-153.

Eupator—His rule extended from about A.D. 154-170.

Sauromates II—From about A.D. 172-210.

Hicetas—A tyrant of Syracuse from 288-279 B.C.

Rhescuporis III—Ruled from about A.D. 211-228.

Cotys III—His rule was from about A.D. 227-234.

Sauromates III—From about A.D. 229-232.

Rhescuporis IV—From about A.D. 233-234.

Inithimeus—Reigned from about A.D. 234-239.

Rhescuporis V—Ruled from about A.D. 239-276.

Sauromates IV—A.D. 275-276.

Pyrrhus—Pyrrhus was a Macedonian who led an expedition into Sicily and probably struck coins while there.

Hieron II—An officer in the army of Pyrrhus. After Pyrrhus left he moved up and ultimately became the ruler of Syracuse. 275-215 B.C.

THE KINGS AND TYRANTS OF SICILY

Gelon—Son of Hieron II.

Agathocles—Ruler of Syracuse in Sicily from 317-289 B.C.

THE KINGS OF SIDON IN PHOENICIA

(Ancient Phoenicia occupied that area which is now Palestine and Lebanon. Sidon was the great seaport of Asia Minor.)

Eshmun' Azar—Possibly a king who ruled Sidon near the end of the fifth century B.C.

Bod' Ashtart—This might have been the king who ruled from 384 to 370 B.C.

Strato I—Ruled from 370-358 B.C.

Tennes—His rule was from 354-348 B.C.

Strato II—Strato was deposed by Alexander the Great. He ruled from 342-333 B.C.

THE KINGS OF SYRIA
(Syria is, of course, in existence today although its borders have changed considerably throughout the ages. The kings listed below were known as the Seleucid kings, deriving the name from the founder of the dynasty, Seleukos I.)

Seleukos I—Seleukos was one of Alexander the Great's generals. Eventually, he seized one part and then another of Alexander's empire until he was ruler of almost all of the Asiatic portion. His rule was from 312-280 B.C. He was known as Nicator.

Antiochos I—Known as SOTER (Savior), he ruled from 280-261 B.C. having, however, associated himself with his father during Seleukos' rule.

Antiochos II—Called THEOS

(god), he ruled with Antiochos I, from about 266-261 B.C. and by himself from 261-246 B.C.

Seleukos II—Ruled from 246-226 B.C.

Antiochos Hierax—A brother of Seleukos II. He led an insurrection against his brother and declared himself king. 246-227 B.C.

Antiochos III—Called the Great, he was another son of Seleukos II and an energetic military leader. His rule covered the period from 223-187 B.C.

Molon—This was a satrap of Media who revolted. He ruled for a year, from 221-220 B.C.

Achaios—A usurper who seized the throne, ruled from 220-214 B.C. then was slain.

Seleukos III—A son of Seleukos II who ruled from 226-223 B.C.

Seleukos IV—His reign was from 187-175 B.C.

Demetrios I—The son of Seleukos IV, he ruled from 162-150 B.C.

Timarchos—Timarchos refused to recognize Demetrios and as satrap of Babylon issued coins in his own name. Ruled about 162 B.C.

Antiochos IV—This was a younger son of Antiochos III who ruled from 175-164 B.C.

Alexander I—Another usurper who ruled from 150-145 B.C.

Antiochos V—Occupied the throne from 164-162 B.C.

Demetrios II—A son of Demetrios I, ruled twice, first from 146 to 140 B.C. when he was captured by the Parthians. When released he ruled from 129-125 B.C.

Antiochos VI—Came to the throne at the age of seven. He was a son of Alexander I and reigned from 145-142 B.C.

Alexander II—Ruled from 128-123 B.C.

Tryphon—Tryphon took the title of Autokratos ("ruler by his own power") after having killed the legitimate ruler. He ruled from 142-139 B.C.

Cleopatra—A fascinating woman who was married at one time or another to three of the Seleukid kings, to Alexander I, Demetrios II, and Antiochos VII. She was guilty of matricide, as well as having had her son Seleukos V murdered. 125-121 B.C.

Antiochos VII—This young brother of Demetrios vanquished Tryphon and ruled from 138-129 B.C.

Antiochos VIII—A son of

Cleopatra. He forced his mother to commit suicide. Actually, she had prepared the poisonous drink for him. He ruled from 121-96 B.C.

Antiochos X—94-83 B.C.

Antiochos IX—After fighting with his half-brother Antiochos VIII, he divided the kingdom taking parts of Phoenicia and Syria for himself. He was a son of Antiochos VII and Cleopatra and ruled from 114-95 B.C.

Seleukos VI—The son of Antiochos VIII, he ruled from 95-94 B.C.

Antiochos XI—A son of Antiochos VIII, he reigned during the year 93 B.C.

Philippus—Also a son of Antiochos VIII. He ruled from 93-83 B.C.

Demetrios III—Another son of the prolific Antiochos VIII. He was king from 95-88 B.C.

Antiochos XII—His reign was from 88-84 B.C. He, too, was a son of Antiochos VIII.

Tigranes II—Tigranes had been king of Armenia and was called into Syria to put an end to the terrible fight for power. He was successful and ruled from 83-69 B.C.

PART II

READING AND DATING
ROMAN
IMPERIAL COINS

by

Zander H. Klawans

Coinage Before the Time
of the Empire

Before discussing the coins of the Roman Empire it is of interest to know a little about the background of these coins and about the development which led to their coming into existence.

One of the Latin words for money is PECUNIA, which originates from the shorter Latin word, PECUS, meaning "cattle." It may not at once be recognized that there is a connection between cattle and money but a brief analysis will show a definite wedding of the two words. Cattle provide sustenance, in one form or another, for humankind. Something with such a universal appeal and of such vital necessity to almost all mankind has positive value. Thus, cattle had value in ancient times. With cattle a man could buy the other necessities of life and wealth could be measured by the number of heads of cattle a man possessed.

Obviously, such bulky material was an inadequate means of exchange. The problems of transporting hundreds of heads of cattle here and there was a great one and it became more intense when the world markets of those days started to blossom; trading in cattle became cumbersomely impossible. The logical answer was the creation of a means of exchange, universally recognized, but small in size. Coinage was the answer.

When Rome first began to flex her muscles and feel the surge of a newborn power, she required and obtained this more flexible system. This first coinage was crude, shapeless and heavy in an attempt to approximate the value of the coin with its actual weight. The first coinage, a cast coinage, was called AES RUDE (rude, or crude bronze. The Latin word for bronze is AES). These first coins probably were cast in the 5th century B.C. They have been found in various shapes, rectangular, flat, square, and in lumps.

Sometime during the third century B.C. a medium of exchange called AES SIGNATUM came into use. These large, cumbersome pieces carried the images of animals, such as birds and cattle upon them, and also inanimate objects, such as tridents and shields. It would seem to be a mistake to call such pieces "money" rather than to consider them as having been used as a means of exchange on the basis of weight.

There next came into existence the coinage which was to be forerunner of all coinage to come. It was called AES GRAVE (heavy bronze) and while it was still a cast coin, it was circular in shape. Some scholars differ as to the exact date this coinage came into existence, but the year 289 B.C. or thereabouts is generally accepted. The AES GRAVE was cast in various denominations. We list them as the AS, the SEMIS, the TRIENS, the QUADRANS, the SEXTANS and the UNCIA. Each of these coins could be distinguished from the other by the obverse (front) of the coin. The AS had the head of the god Janus; the SEMIS pictured Jupiter; the TRIENS, Minerva; the QUADRANS, Hercules; the SEXTANS, Mercury; the UNCIA, Roma. The prow of a ship is found on the reverse of these denominations, undoubetedly indicative of Rome's new found respect for the sea and her turning to the sea and to new lands.

Rome now had to accomplish two things; she had to create a coinage which would be recognized in the land she had conquered or in the land with which she was trading. Thus, it was necessary to emulate the coinage of these countries. Secondly, it was necessary to create a less cumbersome coinage, a coinage which could easily be transported both across the sea and in Italy itself. Both these problems were successfully resolved by the coinage of a silver piece long familiar to the Greeks (and the Romans did inherit from the Greeks) known as the DIDRACHM (or two drachms) and the coinage of copper coins as well. These coins were the first struck coins of Rome (about 280 B.C.)

AS

Janus

Later, probably around 211 B.C., the Romans issued coins which were peculiarly their own. These were the DENARIUS, SESTERTIUS and QUINARIUS. We find coins bearing these same names during the time of the empire, but with the exception of the denarius there is little resemblance between these early coins and the later ones.

Throughout this transition cast coins were still in existence but they were constantly being lowered in weight essentially because of the

SEMIS
Jupiter

TRIENS
Minerva

QUADRANS
Hercules

SEXTANS
Mercury

UNCIA
Roma

REVERSE TYPE

*Prow of
Ship*

inflation which accompanied and followed the Punic Wars, a series of
three wars against the Carthaginians (264-241 B.C.; 218-201 B.C.;
149-146 B.C.). The end of these wars found Rome on the verge of
bankruptcy, a result of which was that the coinage was in a constant
state of flux. The weights of the coins were reduced and all the evils of a
real inflation were in evidence. No one really knew what the money was
worth. However, the final victory of Rome over Carthage in 146 B.C.
led to a gradual but determined reorganization of the coinage and at this
time all coinage was struck; there were no more cast coins. The denarius

emerged as the common coin of the realm and it remained virtually unchanged until the time of the empire. Gold was also struck, but this was in the nature of an emergency and it did not, at this time, form a regular part of the Roman coinage.

It was not long before the coins started to take on a real interest in many ways. There was more of an effort to make them more pleasing from an artistic standpoint. The reverses, in particular, became a media for a multitude of objects of a religious, political, historical and architectural nature. Deities and personifications appeared in great numbers. The coinage had come into its own! There were variances of style and texture to the extent that later-day numismatists would be able to classify these coins both chronologically and geographically.

Roman Coin Denominations

In order to possess a reasonable knowledge of the coins of the Roman Empire it is necessary to know the names by which they are called and to be able to distinguish them from one another.

There were not a great many denominations struck during the period of the Empire and so the beginner should not have too much difficulty in naming them. Certain denominations, such as those struck in gold and some which appeared late in the history of the Empire are quite rare and costly and, therefore, are infrequently seen by the greater majority of collectors. Others are extremely common and it is these coins which form the background of most collections. Probably the most common coins of the period of the Empire are the:

Denarius of Otho

(A.D. 69)

DENARIUS
DUPONDIUS
AS
SESTERTIUS
ANTONINIANUS
FOLLIS

The standard silver coin of the Empire was the DENARIUS. The DENARIUS was first issued about 211 B.C. and remained in existence until about A.D. 296. During this period of years the coin was debased, mostly from the time of the Emperor Nero (A.D. 54-68) onward. At the beginning of the Emperor Caracalla's reign (A.D. 211-217) the DENARIUS was about 40% silver. It was at this time that the ANTONINIANUS appeared.

The ANTONINIANUS derived its name from the Emperor Caracalla (M. Aurelius Antoninus Caracalla, A.D. 211-217) who first introduced it. This coin can be distinguished from the DENARIUS because the head of the subject on the ANTONINIANUS radiate wears a crown. This coin, too, had an auspicious beginning only to be debased to the status of a copper coin with a light silver wash. Occasionally, it is possible to find a late date antoninianus with the silver still present. The coin was abolished at the time of Constantine the Great (A.D. 308-337).

Antoninianus
of
Tacitus
(A.D. 275-276)

The DUPONDIUS was coined during the Imperial period until the time of Trajan Decius (A.D. 249-251). It was struck in brass and is sometimes difficult to distinguish from the AS.

Dupondius
of
Augustus
(29 B.C.-A.D. 14)

One means of determining the difference between the DUPONDIUS and the AS is by the color. The DUPONDIUS is a

As of Domitian
(A.D. 81-96)

rather yellow color, while the AS is more reddish. Occasionally the AS was struck in a brassy metal known as orichalcum. It was usually the practice to strike the DUPONDIUS showing the head of the emperor radiate and the AS with a bare or laureated head.

The SESTERTIUS was the large coin of the empire and is sometimes called a large bronze or grand bronze. Upon the SESTERTIUS appear the most magnificent manifestations of the moneyer's art. The large size of the coin permitted the inclusion of the wonderful detail which was, of a necessity, lacking on the smaller coins. The SESTERTIUS was originally a silver coin of the Roman Republic, worth one quarter of a denarius.

Sestertius
of
Antoninus Pius
(A.D. 138-161)

The Emperor Diocletian (A.D. 284-304) instituted the FOLLIS, which was a rather large coin with a silver wash.

Follis
of
Constantius
(A.D. 305-306)

Other coins, in addition to those mentioned above were the:

AUREUS—The best known of the Roman gold coins. Appeared at about the time of Julius Caesar (45-44 B.C.). The weight of this coin gradually declined until, at the time of Constantine (A.D. 308-337), it was abolished to be replaced by the solidus. The aureus was equal to 25 silver denarii.

CENTENIONALIS—A bronze coin which had its inception during the reign of Constantine (A.D. 308-337). It was bronze with a silver wash. After the time of Arcadius (A.D. 395-408) it sunk into obscurity.

QUADRANS—The fourth part of the AS. Struck in copper.

QUINARIUS—A silver coin about one-half the weight of the denarius. It was issued only at intervals.

SEMIS—These coins were mostly of bronze with very little silver. The coin was issued from the time of the Republic on, and appeared in various sizes and types. It was also used for the Roman half aureus (The aureus was a gold coin). The term SEMISSIS was used to designate the SEMIS when used as a half of the aureus or solidus.

SILIQUA—A Roman silver coin, first issued by Constantine the Great (A.D. 308-337). It was equivalent to 1/24 solidus.

SOLIDUS—A gold coin issued by Constantine the Great (A.D. 308-337).

The Relationship of the Coins to Each Other

The small table which follows will help to distinguish the relationship of the principal coins to each other. The reader will also notice that the larger coins do not necessarily carry the larger value.

Collectors of ancient coins always seem to have been plagued with the question of what a particular coin would have purchased, in terms of the present. Perhaps an answer could be found for a *specific* period in Roman history, although this seems doubtful. We must remember that while a sestertius, for example, might have purchased a loaf of bread during a certain period of Roman history, that same sestertius could not have done so during another period. If we were to study our own monetary system, we would find the same to be true. During inflationary periods, our dollar is worth less than during times of fiscal stability: an automobile may cost four or five times as much as it did 20 or 25 years ago and this would apply to all commodities. The Romans were no different. They, too, went through periods of depression and prosperity, and prosperity with inflation.

Using the denarius as a base, the following relationships prevail:

COIN	NUMBER TO THE DENARIUS
SESTERTIUS	4
DUPONDIUS	8
AS	16
QUADRANS	64

There were, as well, twenty DENARII to the AUREUS, the common gold coin.

PRAENOMEN   NOMEN   COGNOMEN

Before taking up the discussion of the obverse (front) of the Roman coins it would be best first to mention the proper names and the way they are found upon the coins. If it is possible to remember two important facts, the reading of the proper names on the coins should not present a problem.

First: The Roman first name (praenomen) was regularly abbreviated, not by choice but as a designation of Roman citizenship.

Second: The abbreviation "IMP" (Imperator) was regularly used, from the earliest times in the Empire, as a praenomen.

Perhaps the best, and simplest way to describe the terms NOMEN, PRAENOMEN and COGNOMEN is to look to our own usage in present times. The Latin word NOMEN means "name." The prefix, PRAE, means "before". Thus, PRAENOMEN means "before name" or the first name. COGNOMEN is the last name or surname. The Roman name was not a fixed or absolute form. It varied throughout the history of Rome. At first a man was called by one name only. Gradually this was developed into a combination with the genitive case wherein it was then indicated that that person came under the authority of another. A daughter was under the authority of her father; a wife under the authority of her husband; a slave was subservient to his master. And so we would see a name written in this manner: Marcus Marci f (Marcus, the son of Marcus). The single letter "f" designates filius, the Latin word for son. The single letter "f," in the case of a woman would indicate the Latin word filia, daughter.

Explaining the terminology further, instead of saying that the praenomen, nomen and cognomen are the first, middle and last names, respectively, we shall say that the praenomen was the given name, the individual name; the nomen is the name of the gens, or the clan, and the cognomen is the name of the family which is a part of that gens or clan. Thus L. Cornelius Scipio: "L" is the abbreviation of the Latin name Lucius and it is the praenomen, the given name "Cornelius" is the nomen, the name of the gens or clan to which this person's family belongs; "Scipio" is the family name or cognomen. The Scipio family is a part of the Cornelian gens.

Praenomen

The praenomen, as has been mentioned, was strictly the personal name. It was usually conferred by the parents upon the child on the 9th day after birth in the case of boys, and the 8th day after birth in the case of girls. There has been some disagreement on this point because many inscriptions on tombstones have indicated that older boys and girls were nameless and the word "Pupio" (child) appears on many of the stones in the absence of a praenomen.

As stated before the praenomen was regularly abbreviated when used with the nomen and cognomen. This was not a matter of choice but an established custom indicating Roman citizenship. This is a very good point to remember when reading coins, for the praenomina invariably are abbreviated. The following list gives the more common praenomina with their abbreviations:

AULUS.....................A, AU, AUL (rare), O (very rare)
DECIMUS....................D, DEC (rare and late)
CAIUS or GAIUS C
GNAEUS ....CN, GN (very rare)
LUCIUS......................L, LU (rare)
MARCUS.....................M
PUBLIUS.....................P, PUP (rare)
QUINTUS....................Q

```
SERVIUS .........................SER
SERGIUS........................S (rare)
SEXTUS..........................SEX, SX
SPURIUS........................S, SP
TIBERIUS ......................TI
TITUS ...........................T
APPIUS..........................AP, AP P (rare)
NUMERICUS................N
VIBIUS ..........................V
```

The patrician families usually used a particular group of praenomina for all members of their family. A list which might prove to be helpful follows, showing the better known families and the praenomina which they used:

```
AEMILII .........................C, CN, L, MAM, M. Q, TI
CLAUDII........................AP, C, D, L, P. TI, Q
CORNELII.....................A, CN, L, M, P, SER, TI
FABII ............................C, K, M, N, Q
FURII.............................AGRIPPA, C, L, M, SEX, SP
JULII.............................C, L, SEX
MANLII.........................A, CN, L M.
```

Nomen

The nomen is the name which belonged to all members of the same family. At first this name was identified with a certain locality. Later, it was indicative of members of the same gens or clan. The nomen usually ended in "ius," "aius," "eius," "eus." Aemilius, Cornelius, Furius, Manlius and Pompeius are examples.

Cognomen

The cognomen was, at first, a personal name. Later it became a family name, the name of a family within a particular gens or clan. Thus, of the gens Cornelius there were the Cethegi, Lentuli and the Scipiones, to name a few.

Perhaps the clearest way to picture the entire subject of Latin names is to give a present day analogy. The analogy given is a rather "liberal" one, but it shall serve our purpose. Some people carry the maiden name of their mother as a second or "middle" name. Thus, John Scott Pauley, as an example, would show his first name, John (praenomen), the family name of his mother, Scott (nomen), and the name of his own family, Pauley (cognomen). If this example is kept in mind it should be helpful in reading the coins.

The Obverse Inscriptions

There are many methods of collecting Roman coins. Some collections consist of the reverse types; others emphasize a particular reverse type such as the various coins bearing the images of Concordia (Harmony), or Fides (Faith), or of other personifications and deities. Undoubtedly, however, most collections are portrait collections, portraits of the emperors and their contemporaries upon the obverse (front) part of the coin. Perhaps the most interesting is that grouping in which the collector has specialized in the large bronze coins known as sestertii. The large size of this coin enabled the classical engravers to include an abundance of detail which was quite difficult to impress upon coins of smaller dimensions. Any collection, of course, is a matter of the personal taste of the particular collector, and a fine collection of portraits, regardless of the medium used, will make an attractive display.

New collectors experience their greatest difficulty in attempting to read the coins. This is quite interesting because many students of Latin are unable to read the inscriptions simply because of the profusion of abbreviations appearing upon them. Yet, many people who possess fine collections are not students of Latin, and need not be. By remembering certain commonly used abbreviations, a person should be able to read many of the coins which they would come across, provided, of course, that the inscription is legible.

Essentially, the most confusing thing is the habit the Romans possessed of running the entire inscription together with no "break" between the words. A typical inscription appearing upon a sestertius of Nero is an excellent example. For the sake of clarity and simplicity the coin has been subdivided into its logical parts.

Thus, we find we have:

NERO CLAUD CAESAR AUG GER PM TR P IMP PP

If the reader will remember the very few common abbreviations, abbreviations which appear time and time again on almost all the coins of the early empire, the inscription should present no difficulties.

Aug Augustus (or Augusta, if feminine). This was the most distinctive
of all the imperial titles. It was used by no one but the reigning emperor or members of his family. It appears with most frequent regularity on the coins.

PM Another very common title of the emperor.
Pon M Pontifex Maximus was the emperor's title as
Pon Max supreme head of the Roman religion (literally,
Pontifex Max etc. Head priest). The title was held by the emperor
Augustus and all subsequent emperors.

TR P Tribunicia Potestate. The tribunician power. From
Trib P earliest times, the tribunes were the representatives
Trib Pot of the Roman people and, at various times, held
Trib Potest tremendous power. Thus, the Tribunician power
Tribun Potest, etc. represents the emperor's position in that light,
although more specifically, it showed him to be the supreme civil head of the state. The Tr P is quite commonly found with Roman numerals following it. This is an excellent tool to determine the year a particular coin was struck. (A chart is incorporated in this book for the purpose of determining such a date.)

COS COS is the abbreviation for consul. The consul was one of the
two chief magistrates of the Roman state. The emperor himself quite frequently was one of the consuls. When he was not, he usually appointed the person to serve in his place. The COS, as with the TR P, is often followed by Roman numerals. Inasmuch as a consulship lasted for a year, it is also a possible means to determine the date a particular coin was struck by reference to the chart incorporated in this book.

PP PATER PATRIAE. Father of his country. This inscription
appears on many of the coins and was originally a title bestowed upon the emperor by the senate. Some emperors refused the title.

IMP IMPERATOR. Emperor, generally, although the title was
bestowed upon victorious generals in the field during the Republican period and the period of the very early empire. From the time of the emperor Tiberius onward, it was a title used by no one other than the emperor himself.

Now, in looking once more at the above inscription of Nero, we are able to understand the logical breakdown and the complete meaning of the inscription.

1. Nero...His name.

2. Claud...Claudius. The name of the gens to which his family belonged. His nomen.

*3. Caesar...*The inherited name of the Julian family and adopted by the Claudian family. Also adopted by subsequent emperors, and later used by heirs to the throne.

*4. Augustus...*The most distinctive title of the emperor.

*5. Ger...*Germanicus. A hereditary title, as well as a title of honor.

*6. PM...*Pontifex Maximus. The highest priest. The head of the Roman religion.

*7. TR P...*Tribunicia Potestate. The tribunician power. The civil head of state.

*8. IMP...*Imperator. This use of Imperator is as a title of acclamation such as for victories in the field of the emperor of his subordinates.

*9. PP...*Pater Patriae. Father of his country.

Here is another coin, a sestertius of the Emperor Titus. Again, for the sake of convenience, we have subdivided the title.

The complete inscription on the coin

IMP T CAES VESP AUG PM TRP PP COS VIII

Let us again analyze the inscription.

*1. IMP...*Imperator, Emperor.

*2. T...*Titus, his name, or praenomen.

*3. Caes...*Caesar.

*4. Vesp...*Vespasian. The cognomen of the emperor Titus. It was a common practice for an emperor to take as a part of his name the name of his predecessor, particularly if that predecessor had adopted him as his legal heir or if he was the natural heir, as in the case of Titus.

*5. Aug...*Augustus.

6. PM...Pontifex Maximus.

7. TR P...Tribunicia Potestate.

8. PP...Pater Patriae. Father of his country.

9. COS VIII...In his eighth consulship. This coin was struck during the eighth consulship of Titus. Checking with the chart in this book it is indicated that the eighth consulship of Titus occurred in the year AD 80. Thus, the coin pictured here was struck in that year.

As a final example we shall take a coin, an AS, of Domitian. Here again the coin has been struck off into its subdivisions.

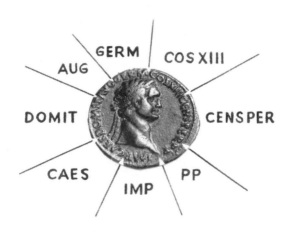

The complete inscription

IMP CAES DOMIT AUG GERM COS XIII CENS PER PP

1. IMP...Imperator. Emperor. Here, however, there is a little different use of the title, for it is used as a praenomen, or a given name.

2. CAES...Caesar.

3. DOMIT...Domitian. His name.

4. AUG...Augustus.

5. GERM...Germanicus.

6. COS XIII...In his 13th consulship. Using the chart in this book, we see that the 13th consulship of Domitian occurred in the year AD 87, the year in which this coin was struck.

7. CENS PER...Censor Perpetuus. The censor was a chief magistrate of the Roman state. The title was quite frequently held by the emperor and was granted for his lifetime. (Thus, the "Perpetuus.")

8. PP... Pater Patriae. Father of his country.

An Alphabetical Check List of the Names of the Emperors as They Frequently Appear on the Coins

This section offers, in alphabetical sequence, the names of the emperors as they appear upon the coins with considerable frequency. The second column presents the names of the emperors as they are commonly known. For example, a coin with the name C CAESAR upon it can be located in the first column. Directly opposite, in the second column, we find that emperor's common name, CALIGULA.

It should be noted that the alphabetical column lists the names exactly as they would appear upon the coin and, as a result, are abbreviated either in part or in whole. For the inquisitive reader, it might be of interest to note the grammatical case differences in some of the names. Most of the names are in the nominative case and yet we find, as in the case of the emperor Trajan, an ending which would not be in the nominative case. TRAIANUS is the nominative ending, but we find the inscription to read, TRAIANO. This is an example of the dative case. Thus, instead of reading, THE EMPEROR TRAJAN AUGUSTUS, etc., as we would expect, it reads, TO...THE EMPEROR TRAJAN AUGUSTUS, etc.

Many times it is difficult to identify the emperor by name alone for some emperors possessed identical names. The photographs of the emperors in the section of this book which includes the biographies should be of some assistance. Gordian I and Gordian II, father and son, had identical names, yet the coins reveal that the elder Gordian had hair well down upon his forehead while the younger Gordian is shown with a bald forehead. Most of the coins of Marcus Aurelius show portraits which are very similar and this should preclude any confusion with other emperors who bore similar titles. Reference to the plates contained in some of the fine volumes which may be found upon the shelves of the larger libraries will supply invaluable assistance in identification. A list of some of the more important works appears in the bibliography at the end of this book.

Name as It Frequently Appears on the Coins   **Common Name**

A

A Vitellius Germanicus	*Vitellius*
Ant Pius Aug	*Caracalla*
Antoninus Aug Pius	*Antoninus Pius*
Antoninus Pius Fel	*Elagabalus*

B

Brittanicus	*Brittanicus*
Brut Imp	*Brutus*

Name as It Frequently Appears on the Coins	Common Name
C	
C Caesar	*Caligula*
C Caesar Aug	*Augustus*
C Iul Verus Maximus	*Maximus*
C M Aur Marius	*Marius*
C Valens Hostil Mes Quintus	*Hostilian*
Caesar	*Julius Caesar*
Caesar Dict	*Julius Caesar*
Constantinus Max Aug	*Constantine the Great*
D	
D Clod Sept	*Clodius Albinus*
D N Ancius Olybrius	*Olybrius*
D N Constantius	*Constantius II*
D N Decentius	*Decentius*
D N Gratianus	*Gratian*
D N Honorius	*Honorius*
D N Iulius Maioranus	*Majorian*
D N Iovianus	*Jovian*
D N Mag Maximus	*Magnus Maximus*
D N Martininianus	*Martinian*
D N Theodosius	*Theodosius I (The Great)*
D N Valentinianus	*Valentinian I*
F	
FI CI Constantinus Iun	*Constantine II*
FI CI Iulianus	*Julian II*
FI CI Hanniballiano Regi	*Hanniballianus*
FI Iul Constans	*Constans*
FI Iul Constantius	*Constantius II*
FI Iul Delmatius	*Delmatius*
FI Nep Constantinus	*Neoptian*
FI Val Constantius	*Constantius I (Chlorus)*
FI Val Severus	*Severus II*
G	
Germanicus Caesar	*Germanicus*
Gal Val Maximianus	*Galerius*
Gal Val Maximinus	*Maximinus II (Gaza)*
H	
Hadrianus Aug	*Hadrian*
I	
Imp T Ael Caes Hadrianus Antoninus	*Antoninus Pius*
Imp Caes Aemilianus	*Aemilian*
Imp D Cl Sep Alb	*Clodius Albinus*

Name as It Frequently Appears on the Coins	Common Name
Imp Sev Alexander	*Severus Alexander*
Imp Antoninus	*Elagabalus*
Imp Caes M Aur Anton	*Caracalla*
Imp Caes M Aurel Antoninus	*Marcus Aurelius*
Imp C L Dom Aurelianus	*Aurelian*
Imp C M Aur Sev Alexander	*Severus Alexander*
Imp C D Cael Balbinus	*Balbinus*
Imp C Carausius	*Carausius*
Imp C M Aur Carus	*Carus*
Imp C Claudius	*Claudius II*
Imp Caes D Cl Sep Alb	*Clodius Albinus*
Imp Constantinus	*Constantine the Great*
Imp Caes M Did Sever Iulian	*Didius Julianus*
Imp C Diocletianus	*Diocletian*
Imp Caes Domit	*Domitian*
Imp Cl Domitius Domitianus	*Domitius Domitianus*
Imp C M An Florianus	*Florianus*
Imp Ser Galba Aug	*Galba*
Imp C D Lic Gallienus	*Gallienus*
Imp Caes P Sept Geta	*Geta*
Imp Caes M Ant Gordianus	*Gordian I and II*
Imp Gordianus Pius	*Gordianus Pius (III)*
Imp C Laelianus	*Laelianus*
Imp C Val Licin Licinius	*Licinius I*
Imp C Ful Macrianus	*Macrianus II*
Imp C M Opel Macrinus	*Macrinus*
Imp Caes Magnentius	*Magnentius*
Imp C Maxentius	*Maxentius*
Imp C M A Maximianus	*Maximianus I (Hercules)*
Imp Maximinus Pius Aug	*Maximinus I*
Imp Nero Caes	*Nero*
Imp Nerva Caes	*Nerva*
Imp M Otho Caes	*Otho*
Imp Ti Cl Mar Pacatian	*Pacatian*
Imp Caes P Helv Pertinax	*Pertinax*
Imp Caes C Pescennius Niger	*Pescennius Niger*
Imp Philippus Aug	*Philip I*
Imp M Iul Philippus	*Philip I*
Imp C Postumus	*Postumus*
Imp C Probus	*Probus*
Imp Caes Pupien	*Pupienus*
Imp C M Clod Pupienus	*Pupienus*
Imp C Ful Quietus	*Quietus*
Imp C P C Regalianus	*Regalianus*

Name as It Frequently Appears on the Coins   Common Name

Imp C M Aur Sev Alexander .... *Severus Alexander*
Imp Sev Alexander .... *Severus Alexander*
Imp C M CI Tacitus .... *Tacitus*
Imp C Tetricus... *Tetricus I*
Imp Traiano Aug.. *Trajan*
Imp Caes Nervae Traiano .... *Trajan*
Imp Traianus Decius..................................... *Trajan Decius*
Imp C C Trebonianus Gallus .... *Trebonianus Gallus*
Imp Caes L Aurel Verus .... *Lucius Verus*
Imp Caes Vesp .... *Vespasian*
Imp T Caes Vesp... *Titus*
Imp C Piav Victorinus .... *Victorinus*
Imp Cae C Vib Volusiano .... *Volusian*

L
L Aelius Caesar .... *Aelius*
L Aurel Commodus .... *Commodus*
L Iul Aur Sulp Ura Antoninus........................ *Uranius Antoninus*
L Sept Sev .... *Septimius Severus*
L Septimius Geta Caes .... *Geta*
Licinius Iun .... *Licinius II*

M
M Agrippa .... *Agrippa*
M Antoni... *Marc Antony*
M Aur Anton Caes... *Caracalla*
M Aur Carinus.. *Carinus*
M Aur Numerianus .... *Numerian*
M Commodus Antoninus............................... *Commodus*
M Lepidus .... *Lepidus*
M Opel Antoninus Diadumenianus................. *Diadumenian*
Mag Decentius.. *Decentius*
Magnus Pius .... *Pompey the Great*
Maximinus Pius Aug Germanicus .... *Maximinus I*

N
Nero Caes Aug.. *Nero*
Nero Claudius Caesar .... *Nero*
Nero Claudius Drusus .... *Nero Claudius Drusus*

P
P Sept Geta Caes... *Geta*

Q
Q Her Etr Mes Decius .... *Herennius Etruscus*

S
Ser Galba Imp Caes .... *Galba*

Name as It Frequently
Appears on the Coins　　　　　　**Common Name**

T

T Caes Imp..*Titus*
Ti Caes Augustus ....*Tiberius*
Ti Claud Caes...*Claudius*

The Informal and Formal Names
of the Emperors

As an additional aid, and in order to provide additional information, the following two columns present, first, the informal or common names of the emperors and some of their contemporaries and, in the second column, their formal names.

Common Name　　　　　**Full Name**

Aelius...Lucius Aelius Verus Caesar
Aemilian...Marcus Aemilius Aemilianus
Agrippa...Marcus Vipsania Agrippa
Antoninus Pius...Titus Aelius Hadrianus Antoninus
Augustus Octavian...Caius Iulius Caesar Octavianus
Aurelian...Lucius Domitius Aurelianus

Balbinus...Decimus Caelius Balbinus
Brutus...Marcus Iunius Brutus
Britannicus...Tiberius Claudius Britannicus

Caligula...Caius Caesar
Caracalla...Marcus Aurelius Antoninus
Carausius...Marcus Aurelius Mausaeus Carausius
Carus...Marcus Aurelius Carus
Claudius...Tiberius Claudius Drusus
Claudius II...Marcus Aurelius Claudius
Clodius Albinus...Decimus Clodius Ceionius Septimius Albinus
Constans...Flavius Iulius Constans
Constantine the Great...Flavius Valerius Constantinus
Constantine II...Flavius Claudius Iulius Constantinus
Constantius I (Chlorus)...Flavius Valerius Constantius
Constantius II...Flavius Iulius Constantius

Decentius...Magnus Decentius
Delmatius...Flavius Iulius Delmatius
Diadumenian...Marcus Opelius Antoninus Diadumenianus
Didius Julianus...Marcus Didius Salvius Iulianus
Diocletian...Caius Valerius Diocletianus
Domitian...Titus Flavius Domitianus
Domitius Domitianus...Lucius Domitius Domitianus

Elagabalus...Marcus Aurelius Antoninus

Common Name	Full Name

Florian...Marcus Annius Florianus

Galba...Servius Sulpicius Galba
Galerius...Galerius Valerius Maximianus
Gallienus...Publius Licinius Valerianus Egnatis Gallienus
Germanicus...Germanicus
Geta...Lucius (or Publius) Septimius Geta
Gordian I and III (Pius)...Marcus Antonius Gordianus
Gordian II...Marcus Antonianus Gordianus
Gratian...Flavius Gratianus

Hadrian...Publius Aelius Hadrianus
Hanniballianus...Flavius Claudius Hanniballianus
Herennius Etruscus...Quintus Herennius Etruscus Messius Decius
Honorius...Flavius Honorius
Hostilian...Caius Valens Hostilianus Messius Quintus

Jovian...Flavius Claudius Iovianus
Julius Caesar...Caius Iulius Caesar
Julian I...Marcus Aurelius Iulianus
Julian II...Flavius Claudius Iulianus

Laelianus...Ulpius Cornelius Laelianus
Lepidus...Marcus Aemilius Lepidus
Licinius I...Publius Flavius Galerius Valerius Licinianus Licinius
Licinius II...Flavius Valerius Licinianus Licinius

Macrianus I...Marcus Fulvius Macrianus
Macrianus II...Titus Fulvius Iulius Macrianus
Macrinus...Marcus Opelius Severus Macrinus
Magnentius...Flavius Magnus Magnentius
Magnus Maximus...Magnus Clemens Maximus
Majorian...Iulianus Maiorianus
Marc Antony...Marcus Antonius
Marcus Aurelius...Marcus Aelius Aurelius Verus
Marius...Caius Marcus Aurelius Marius
Martinian...Marcus Martinianus
Maxentius...Marcus Aurelius Valerius Maxentius
Maximianus I...Marcus Aurelius Valerius Maximianus
Maximinus I...Caius Iulius Verus Maximinus
Maximinus II(Daza)...Galerius Valerius Maximinus

Nepotian...Flavius Popilius Nepotianus Constantinus
Nero...Nero Claudius Caesar Drusus Germanicus
Nero Claudius Drusus...Nero Claudius Drusus
Nerva...Marcus Cocceius Nerva
Numerian...Marcus Aurelius Numerianus

Olybrius...Ancius Olybrius
Otho...Marcus Salvius Otho

Pacatian...Tiberius Claudius Marinus Pacatianus

Common Name	Full Name
Pertinax...Publius Helvius Pertinax	
Pescennius Niger...Caius Pescennius Niger	
Philip I...Marcus Iulius Philippus	
Pompey the Great...Cnaeus Pompeius Magnus	
Postumus...Marcus Cassianius Latimius Postumus	
Probus...Marcus Aurelius Probus	
Pupienus...Marcus Clodius Pupienus Maximus	

Quietus...Fulvius Julius Quietus

Regalianus...Publius Caius Regalianus

Saturninus...Sextus Iulius Saturnninus
Septimius Severus...Lucius Septimius Severus
Severus Alexander...Marcus Aurelius Severus Alexander
Severus II...Flavius Valerius Severus
Sextus Pompey...Sextus Pompeius Magnus

Tacitus...Marcus Claudius Tacitus
Tetricus I...Caius Pius Esuvius Tetricus
Theodosius I (The Great)...Flavius Theodosius
Theodosius II...Flavius Theodosius
Tiberius...Tiberius Claudius Nero
Titus...Titus Flavius Sabinus Vespasianus
Trajan...Marcus Ulpius Traianus
Trajan Decius...Caius Messius Quintus Traianus Decius
Trebonianus Gallus...Caius Vibius Trebonianus Gallus

Uranius Antoninus...Lucius Iulius Aurelius Sulpicius Uranius Antoninus

Valentinian I...Flavius Valentinianus
Valentinian II...Flavius Valentinianus
Valentinian III...Plocidius Valentinianus
Vespasian...Titus Flavius Sabinus Vespasianus
Victorinus...Marcus Piavvonius Victorinus
Vitellius...Aulus Vitellius
Volusian...Caius Vibius Volusianus Trebonianus Gallus

The Reverse Figures on Roman Coins
(Deities and Personifications)

The variety of figures on the reverse of the coins is a subject of more than passing interest. The types are numerous and a partial list is included here. Many of the coins picture a deity (Roman god or goddess) or a personification. A personification is the personalizing of a place or thing. Concordia, as an example is the personalizing of a thing, concord or harmony; Fortuna is the personification of fortune, and so on. Frequently, a figure may be identified by carefully observing its dress, the objects held by the figure or the position of the figure itself.

For example, it will be noted that Spes, the personification of "hope," is usually found walking, holding a flower and slightly lifting her skirt. A coin with this personification upon it would need no spelled-out description, for no other figure is represented in a similar manner. Hercules, a deity, appears as a powerful man, wearing a lion skin, and with a club in his hand. As such, he should easily be recognizable.

The reader should remember that all inscriptions appearing on the reverses do not necessarily refer to, or identify the figure.

Deities

Aesculapius

AESCULAPIUS—The god of Medicine and ofhealing. He is shown holding a staff about which a serpent twines (the insignia of the medical profession.) He is sometimes accompanied by a small figure, Telesphorus, his attendant.

Apollo

APOLLO—The Sun god and god of Music and the Arts. He usually has the title Conservator, or Palatinus (Protector of the imperial residence on the Palatine) or Moneta (deity of the mint). He is usually holding a lyre.

Ceres

CERES—The goddess of Agriculture. Usually holding ears of corn, and frequently a torch.

Cybele

CYBELE—The mother of the gods. Usuallywears a crown and is in a car drawn by lions or sits on a throne between lions.

Diana

DIANA—The Moon-goddess. Sometimes has a crescent of the moon above her head, or bow and arrows, accompanied by hounds or deer. Occasionally given the title of torch bearer (Lucifera) and holds a torch. Other titles are Conservatrix, Ephesia, and Victrix.

HERCULES—Representing Strength. Recognizable by his excellent physique and the club and lion skin.

Hercules

JANUS—A double-headed deity often seen on Roman Republican coinage but infrequently appearing on imperatorial coins. He was the god of the past and future (looking both ways).

Janus

JUPITER—Also Jove or Optimus Maximus (the Best and Highest or Greatest). Appears nude or semi-nude, with a full beard. Holds a thunderbolt in his right hand and a scepter in his left. He was the father of the gods. The titles are different on the coins. On some he is called Conservator (the Conservator of the emperor or of the state), or Tonans (the thunderer), or Stator (the stayer of armies about to flee).

Jupiter

Juno

JUNO—The wife of Jupiter. She holds a patera (a small dish used in Roman days for drinking or for the pouring of libations) and a scepter. Many times she is accompanied by a peacock. Some of her titles are Regina (Queen), Lucina (as deity of childbirth), Conservatrix and Victrix.

Liber

LIBER—Bacchus. Liber is his Italian name. Usually holds a wine cup and a staff surmounted by a pine cone or a bunch of grapes (thyrsus) and accompanied by a panther.

Mars

MARS—The god of War. Shown, usually, with shield and spear, and is often nude with the exception of a helmet. Also, sometimes shown with a trophy instead of a shield. Some of his titles are Propugnator (fighter... for Rome), or Ultor (the Avenger). With the title Pacifer (Pacifier) he bears the olive branch representing peace.

MERCURY—The Messenger of the gods. Usually wears a winged cap (petasus) and carries a purse and caduceus. Some of his titles are Pacifer and Conservator.

Mercury

MINERVA—Goddess of Wisdom, Patroness of the Arts and the hope of men in war. She usually wears a shield and spear, and a helmet. Some of her titles are Pacifera and Victrix.

Minerva

Neptune

NEPTUNE—God of the Sea. Usually holds a trident and a dolphin. The prow of a galley is sometimes included and many coin-types show him with his foot upon the prow.

ROMA—The goddess of Rome. Usually helmeted and in armor. Holds a small figure of Victory at times, or a wreath, or a parazonium (a small sword or dagger).

Roma

Sol

SOL—The Sun-god. Usually nude with a radiate head, holding a whip or a globe. Sometimes he is shown in a chariot or with the horses of the sun included. His titles include Comes, Invictus, or, less frequently, Oriens (the rising or eastern sun).

Venus

VENUS—The goddess of Love. Usually completely clothed or almost so. Some of her apparel includes an apple, or the helmet of Mars and a scepter. Sometimes accompanied by Cupid. Her titles include, Coelestis (heavenly), Felix (happy), Genetrix and Victrix.

Vesta

VESTA—Goddess of "family life." Shown as a matron holding a patera and scepter. Her titles include Sancta (holy) and Mater (mother).

The Three Graces

VULCAN—God of Fire and Iron. The Iron-Monger of the gods. Usually shown with the tools of the blacksmith's trade.

THE THREE GRACES—Euphrosyne, Aglaia and Thalia. Lesser deities who presided over the banquet, the dance and all social enjoyments and elegant arts. The three appear together.

Personifications

ABUNDANTIA — Abundance, plenty. Holds ears of corn and cornucopiae (Horn of Plenty).

Abundantia

AEQUITAS — Fair dealing, equity. Holds scales and cornucopiae.

Aequitas

AETERNITAS — Eternity, stability. Holds torch, globe or scepter, or the heads of the sun and the moon.

Aeternitas

ANNONA — Corn harvest. Holds ears of corn and cornucopiae and is usually shown with the prow of a galley symbolizing the necessity of having corn shipped into Rome for its sustenance.

Annona

Clementia

BONUS EVENTUS — Good luck, good fortune. A masculine personification. Holds patera over altar, and a cornucopiae.

CLEMENTIA — Mercy, clemency. Holds branch and scepter, and sometimes leans upon a column.

Concordia

CONCORDIA — Harmony, concord. Holds scepter, patera or cornucopiae.

Felicitas

FELICITAS — Happiness, prosperity. Holds cornucopiae and caduceus.

FIDES — Good faith, confidence. Holds patera and cornucopiae, or ears of corn and basket of fruit. As Fides Militum, holds two standards or other evidence of a military nature.

Fides

FORTUNA — Fortune. Holds rudder and cornucopiae. At times shown resting on globe. May also hold olive branch or patera.

Fortuna

HILARITAS — Rejoicing, mirth. Holds cornucopiae and long palm. Sometimes two small children are shown and frequently one child.

Hilaritas

HONOS — Honor. A masculine personification. Holds olive branch or scepter, and cornucopiae.

Honos

INDULGENTIA — Indulgence, mercy. Holds patera and scepter.

Indulgentia

205

Justitia

JUSTITIA — Justice. Holds olive branch or patera and scepter. Infrequently she is seen holding scales.

Laetitia

LAETITIA — Joy. Holds wreath and scepter, or occasionally a rudder on a globe in place of the scepter. She may rest her hand on an anchor.

Liberalitas

LIBERALITAS — Liberality. Holds tablet(tessera) and cornucopiae.

Libertas

LIBERTAS — Liberty, freedom. Holds a pointed cap of liberty (pileus) and scepter.

MONETA —Money, mint. Holds scales and cornucopiae. Sometimes three figures appear, as pictured.

Moneta

PATIENTIA — Patience, endurance. Holds scepter.

Pax

PAX — Peace. Holds olive branch and scepter or cornucopiae.

Pietas

PIETAS — Piety, dutifulness. Quite frequently veiled. Holds patera and scepter. Sometimes is shown sacrificing at the altar.

Providentia

PROVIDENTIA — Providence. Holds baton and scepter. Occasionally a globe appears at her feet.

Pudicitia

PUDICITIA — Chastity, modesty. Usually shown veiled, holding scepter.

Salus

SALUS — Health, welfare, safety. Holds patera from which she feeds a serpent coiled around an altar. Sometimes she is found holding the serpent in her arms and feeding it.

Securitas

SECURITAS — Security, confidence. Holds scepter or patera.

SPES — Hope. Holds flower. Is usually walking, slightly lifting her skirt.

Spes

UBERITAS — Fertility. Holds cornucopiae and purse.

Uberitas

Victoria

VICTORIA — Victory, winged. Holds wreath and palm. May be bearing a shield or may be writing upon a shield or erecting a trophy. (The process of erecting a trophy was an ancient one and symbolized victory over the enemy in the field.)

VIRTUS — A masculine personification for courage. Usually shown in complete armor holding Victory and a spear, or a spear and a shield.

Virtus

The Reverse Inscriptions on Roman Coins

The list or inscriptions included here is presented for the purpose of giving the reader a small cross section of the manifold varieties in existence. A complete list may be found in H. Cohen's *Description historique des monnais frappées sous l'Empire romain*. Quite frequently the value of a particular coin is determined by the reverse, for some reverses are much rarer than others.

Many of the coins are without inscriptions of any kind with the exception of the letters SC (on coins of the early empire, and figures representing deities or personifications. The letters SC mean Senatus Consulto, by decree of the senate. The senate had under its control the minting of all copper and bronze coins, while the emperor had control over those struck in silver and gold. Practically speaking, this was merely a concession granted to the senate by the emperor, for he was supreme in every sense of the word, and remained so until the armies realized, only too quickly, that the elevation of an emperor was completely within their hands. Thus, SC is a symbol, true, but a symbol which should not be taken too literally despite its universal use upon the coins.

The various combinations of inscriptions are exceedingly numerous. By "combination" it is meant the various adjectives which are used to describe the many different personalities. In the instance of Mars, we find:

Mars Victor		Mars the Victor
Marti Conservatori	(to)	Mars the Conservator
Marti Pacifer	(to)	Mars the Pacifier
Marti Propugnatori	(to)	Mars the Defender
Mars Ultor		Mars the Avenger

These same adjectives are used to describe other deities or personifications. Thus, for Jupiter we find, to name a few:

Iovi Conservatori	(to)	Jupiter the Conservator
Iovi Statori	(to)	Jupiter the Stabilizer or Provider
Iovi Propugnatori	(to)	Jupiter the Defender

In the later empire certain symbols became quite common. Among these are the abbreviated forms, singular and plural, of the words Dominus Noster (Our Lord, but in the liberal sense meaning our lord and ruler, of the Roman people). The symbol D N, therefore, means Dominus Noster in one grammatical case or another. D D N N is the plural for D N and indicates two rulers or more. N N would be the plural for the word "our."

Thus,

    Victoria Aeterna Augg NN...Eternal Victory of OUR emperors

The same interesting method of describing pluralities would apply in the case of the abbreviation AUG or CAES. Two rulers would be indicated by adding another "g" to the end of AUG. This would then show on the coin as AUGG. The same is true for the designation of Caesar. Two Caesars would be shown as CAESS. It was an excellent means of conserving space on the coin.

The inscriptions which follow are exactly as they appear on certain coins. This means that all or part of the inscription is abbreviated. It will be noted that many words which appear to the eye to be the same possess different endings. This is due to the exact use of the word within the inscription itself.

The endings are changed because of a change of grammatical case. And so Rome, in Latin, may appear as Romanorum, the genitive (possessive) case, or as Roma, the nominative case, depending upon its use. Venus, is the nominative case while Veneris, denotes the genitive (possessive) case. Keeping these examples in mind should prevent a considerable amount of confusion.

Finally, many of the inscriptions we are accustomed to observe on the obverse of the coin appear upon the reverse of quite a few coins. We find TR P, COS, PM, PP and others appearing as part of reverse inscriptions. In some instances the above are carried over from the obverse in order to complete the inscription.

The INSCRIPTIONS are printed in *Italic Type*.
Their LIBERAL MEANINGS are printed in Regular Type.

Inscription   **Liberal Meaning**
Advent Aug (or Augg)...Arrival of the emperor or emperors.
Adventui Aug Felicissimo...Refers to the felicitations of the
   Roman people upon the return of the emperor.
Aeternae memoriae...(to) Eternal remembrance.
Apolloni Sancto...(to) Holy Apollo.
Beata tranquillitas...Blessed Peace (of the state).
Bono Genio Pii Imperatoris...(to) the good Genius of the emperor.
Bonus Eventus...Good events or happenings.
Cereri Frugif...(to) The fruit-bearing Ceres.
Claritas Reipub...Brightness of the Republic.
Clementia Temp...Clemency of the emperor (at the time).
Colonia Bostra...Colony of Bostra (Arabia).
Concord Aequit...Concord of Equity.
Concordia Augg...Concord of the emperors.
Concord Mili or Concordia Militum...Military concord.
Conserv Urb Suae...Conserver of the city (Rome).
Comiti Augg NN...Retinue of the emperors.
Dacia...A country.
Deo Vulcano...(to) The god Vulcan.
Diana Lucifera...Diana the bringer of light.
Dis Genitalibus...For having children.

Inscription	Liberal Meaning

D N Licini Augusti...(of) our lord Licinius, emperor.

Dominor Nostror Caess...Caesars our lords.

Erculi Victori...To Hercules the Victor.

EX S.C. Ob Cives Servatos...A decree of the senate bestowed for having saved the lives of citizens.

Fecund Augustae...Fertility of the Empress.

Fel Temp Reparatio...Restoration of the happy times.

Felicitas Augg NN...Happiness of our emperors.

Felicitas Reipublicae...Happiness of the Republic.

Felix Advent Augg NN...Happy arrival of both our emperors.

Fides Exerc or Fides Exercitum...Fidelity of the soldiers or of the army.

Fides Mutua Augg...Mutual faith of the emperors.

Fort Red or Fortuna Redux...Fortunate return of our emperor.

Fortunae Reduci Augg N N...(to) the fortunate return of our emperors.

Genio Antiocheni...Genius (Guardian) of Antioch.

Genio Augg et Caesarum NN...(to) the genius of the emperors and our Caesars.

Genio Augusti, Genio Imperatoris...(to) the genius of the emperor (or emperors).

Genio Pop Rom...(to) the genius of the Roman people.

Genius Senatus...Genius of the senate.

Germania...A country, province.

Gloria Novi Saeculi...The glory of the new age.

Gloria Romanorum...The glory of Rome. (Of the Romans.)

Hilaritas Augg...Mirth or joy of our emperors.

Hoc Signo Victor Eris...By this sign shalt thou be the victor (or shalt thou conquer).

Honos...Honor.

Honos et *Virtus*...Honor and virtue.

Indulgentia Augg In Carth...Indulgence of the emperors to Carthage.

Iovi Conservator Augg NN...(to) Jupiter, conservator of our emperors.

Iov Exsup, etc....Jove (Jupiter) who excels in all things.

Iovi Propugnatori...(to) Jupiter the defender.

Iovi Statori...(to) Jupiter the stabilizer.

Iovi Vot Susc Pro Sal Caes Aug SPQR...Vows to Jupiter by the senate and the Roman people for the restoration of the health of the emperor.

Iul....Julius or Julia.

Iun....Junior.

Iuno Felix...Happy Juno.

Iuno Lucina...Goddess of light.

Iuno Regina...Juno the Queen.

Iunoni Martiali...(to) the war-like Juno.

Iuppitor Custos...Jupiter the custodian.

Iustitia...Justice.

Iuventus Augustus...The young Augustus.

Inscription	Liberal Meaning

Isis Faria...Isis, protectress of the Island of Pharos.

Laetit Fundata, Laetitia Fund...Well founded rejoicing.

Leg I, Leg II, Leg III, etc....The numbers of the legions.

Lib Aug, etc....Liberality of the emperor.

Mag Pius...Great and pious.

Mars Ultor...Mars, the avenger.

Mars Victor...Mars, the victor.

Mart Pac, Mati Pacif or Pacifero...Mars, the pacifier.

Martia Conservatori...(to) Mars, the conserver.

Marti Propugt...(to) Mars, the defender.

Mauretania...A province.

Miliarum Saeculum...Commencement of the new era or age.

Miner Fautr...Minerva who gives favors.

Moneta Aug...Money of the emperor.

Munificentia Aug...Munificence of the emperor.

N.F....Nobilissima Femina (Most noble woman).

Oriens Aug....Rising sun (of the emperor).

Pacator Orbis...Pacifier of the earth.

Pace Pr Ubiq Parta Ianum Clusit...Refers to the portal of Janus
   being closed, indicating peace.

Paci Augustae...To the peace of the emperor.

Par, Ar Ad, etc...Parthia, Arabia Adiabenius (conquered nations).

Pax Fundata Cum Persis...Firm peace with the Persians.

Pietas Mutua Aug...The mutual piety of the two Augusti.

Pietas Romana...Roman piety.

Popul Iussu...By order of the Roman people.

Primi Decennales...(of the) First period of ten years.

Profectio Aug...The emperor setting out for a visit or expedition.

Prov Deor, Provid Deor, Providentia Deorum...Providence of the gods.

Providentiae Caess...Foresight of the Caesars.

Rector Orbis...Master of the world.

Regi Artis...(To the) King of the Arts.

Relig Aug...Religion of the emperor.

Reliqua Vetera H S Novies Mill Abolita...Refers to the liberality of the
   emperor (Hadrian) in remitting debts.

Reparatio Reipub...Restoration of the Republic.

Restitutor Africae...Restitutor or ruler of Africa.

Restitutor Orbis...Restitutor or ruler of the world.

Restitutor Urbis...Restitutor or ruler of the city.

Sac Mon Urb Augg et Caes N N or Sacra Monet Augg et Caes Nostr....Sacred
   money of Rome, our emperors and our Caesars.

Saec Fel...Happy Age.

Saeculi (or Seculi) Felicitas...Happy Age (also refers to the secular games).

Saeculo Frugifero...(to) The fruitful age.

Saeculum Novum...The new age.

Inscription	Liberal Meaning

Sal Gen Hum...Salus Generis Humani (Lasting health to all humans).

Salus DD NN Aug et Caes...The health of Augustus and Caesar, our lords.

Salus Reipublicae...The health of the Republic.

Sanct Deo Soli Elagabal...(to) Holy Sun-God Elagabalus.

Sarmatia Devicta...Victory over Sarmatia.

Securit Imperii...Security of the empire.

Securit Perp...Eternal security.

Serapi Comiti Aug...(to) Serapis, Companion and god of the emperor.

Soli Invicto Comiti...(to) The unconquerable Sun-God.

Senatus Populusque Romanus...The senate and the Roman people.

SPQR Optimo Principi...The senate and the Roman people to the highest prince.

Spes Perpetua...Eternal hope.

Spes Romanorum...Hope of the Romans.

Summus Sacerdos Aug...Highest prince (or priest) Augustus.

Tempor Felix ...The happy times.

Tiberis...The Tiber (A personification).

Ubertas...Fertility.

Undique Victores...Victory everywhere.

Urbs Roma Felix...The happy city, Rome.

Veneri Victrici...(to) Venus the Victress.

Venus Coelestis...Heavenly Venus.

Venus Felix...Happy Venus.

Victoria Aeterna Aug N...Eternal Victory for our emperor.

Victoriae D D Augg N N...(to) Victory of our emperors.

Virtus Exerciti...Referring to the courage of the army.

Virtus Militum...Victory (Virtue) of the army.

Virtus Romanorum...Virtue of the Romans.

Vot Susc or Vota Suscepta...Sacrifice vows.

Votis Decennalibus...Vows of the ten years or the tenth year.

Vota Publica...Public vows.

Mint Marks

Roman coins began to carry mint marks around the middle of the third century A.D. With the use of these mint marks the emperor had reasonably strict control over the actions of the mint officials. Coins of inadequate weight (perhaps indicating that a mint official was filling his personal purse) were then easily traced to the guilty person or persons.

The mint mark is found in the exergue (bottom) of the reverse. Generally it consists of three parts: a letter indicating pecunia (P), money or SM (Sacred money) or M (Moneta). The next letter or letters would indicate the place where the coin was struck. (ROM, Rome; SIR, Sirmium; etc.) Last, the symbol, either in Greek or Latin, indicating the workshop in that particular place. As an example, if the Greek system was used, the first letters of the Greek alphabet (Alpha, Beta, Gamma, etc.) would be found upon the coin, indicating the particular workshop. Workshop number 1 would be Alpha; workshop number 2, Beta; and so on. The Latin system would be used in exactly the same manner and so prima would be workshop number 1; secunda, workshop number 2; tertia, workshop number 3. The symbols, in this instance, would be "P" for prima, "S" for secunda, "T" for tertia, and "Q" for quarta.

The following list includes some of the more common mints. The names of modern towns appear in parentheses.

Alexandria *(Egypt)*...AL, ALE, ALEX, SMAL
Ambianum *(Amiens, France)*...AMB, AMBI.
Antioch *(Antikiya, Syria)*...AN, ANT. ANTOB.
Aquileia *(Aquileia, Italy)*...AQ, AQVI, SMAQ.
Arelatum *(Arles, France)*...AR, ARL, CONST.
Camulodunum *(Colchester, Eng.)*...C, CL.
Carthage *(Ruins near Tunis, North Africa)*...K, KAR, KART.
Constantinople *(Istanbul, Turkey)*...C, CON, CONS, CONOB.
Cyzicus *(Kapu Dagh, Turkey)*...CUZ, CUZIC, CYZ, CYZIC,
   K, KV, KVZ, KY, SMK.
Heraclea *(Eregli, Turkey)*...H, HER, HERACL, HT, SMH.
Londinium *(London)*...L, Ll, LN, LON, PLON.
Lugdunum *(Lyons, France)*...LD, LG, LUG, LUGD.
Mediolanum *(Milan, Italy)*...MD, MED, MDOB.
Nicomedia *(Izmit, Turkey)*...N, NIC, NICO, NIK, SMN.
Ostia *(The port of Rome)*...OST.
Ravenna *(Ravenna, Italy)*...RAV, RVPS.
Rome...R, RM, ROM, ROMA, URB ROM.
Serdica *(Sophia, Bulgaria)*...SD, SER, SERD.
Sirmium *(Ruins near Mitrovica, Yugoslavia)*...SIR, SIRM, SM.
Siscia *(Sisak, Yugoslavia)*...S, SIS, SISC.
Thessalonica *(Salonika, Greece)*...TE, TES, TESOB, TH, TS, OES.
Ticinum *(Pavia, Italy)*...T.
Treveri *(Trier, Germany)*...TR, TRE, TROB.

Solidus
Struck in
Constantinople

Note CONS in exergue (bottom) of coin illustrated.

Chronological Sketches
of the Emperors,
Their Contemporaries and Families

Any attempt to tell the story of Rome's Emperors in as brief a manner as is here presented is obviously quite inadequate. However, these little sketches should be of benefit for a hurried background to the collector who is not familiar with the history of Rome. The coins themselves, after all, are but little metal manifestations of the greater story, the story of Rome itself.

It is impossible to escape the joy, tragedy, violence, and the monumental egoism of the people whose hands guided the destinies of millions of Romans.

We read of the tragedy of the emperor-father who committed suicide upon learning of the death of his son in battle (Gordianus Africanus.) The moral concept of our time forces us to cringe at the alleged sins of Tiberius or the insane depravity of Caligula, who thought to make his horse Consul. The great promise which Domitian showed in his early years turned into a disappointing performance of excessive corruption. How did the pupil of the philosopher Seneca (Nero) learn his lessons to become so imbued with evil that he destroyed almost everyone who surrounded him including the mother whose wiles had elevated him to his high position (Agrippina), and a wife (Poppaea?) Even his teacher suffered a similar fate. Assassination, here, reached a high artistic standard.

Do we understand this woman who was mother of an emperor, wife of an emperor and sister of an emperor? Her ambition brought her the ultimate in every material phase but her actions disgusted even her dissolute son whom she had made emperor. He ordered her to be poisoned (Agrippina, mother of Nero, wife of the emperor Claudius, sister of the emperor Caligula.)

How low the tides of government had sunk when that very government had to be auctioned to the person who was the highest bidder. Didius Julianus achieved this dubious distinction only to meet a violent death shortly thereafter. And the emperor Marius; little is known of him because he ruled for about two or three days. There was a child-emperor, too. Valentinianus II was proclaimed emperor at the age of 3, not an age to be able to decide whether such a title was to his advantage. He was murdered in his twentieth year.

We read about the boy-ruler Elagabalus. Emperor at the age of 14 and 4 years later dragged, dead, through the streets of Rome to be thrown into the Tiber. Despite his extreme youth he rapidly matured in the fine art of vicious cruelty.

We wonder about the man, Vitellius, who thought enough of the throne to wage battle for it but who, upon achieving his ambition, concerned himself more with the luxuries of his table. His fate was to be seized in his palace and to be dragged ignominiously through the streets of Rome to be killed by the mob.

What do we say of Commodus? Commodus, the son of the noble and good Marcus Aurelius; Commodus, in whom the sons of Rome had absolute faith that the excellent government of his father would be continued. He answered this faith placed in him by a rule of terror, evil and corruption. Fate kept an accurate record, however, and his last moments were ruthlessly pressed out of him as he died by strangulation at the hands of an underling.

Fratricide was the peculiar talent possessed by Caracalla. It did not please him to have to share the empire with his brother Geta although it was his father's expressed wish that he do so. And so he had his brother murdered. As if this were not enough he ordered, in addition, that all effigies of his brother on monuments and coins be destroyed. That this was not carried out is indicated by the existence of an abundance of coins of Geta. Caracalla was, himself, murdered.

Yet, there are softer pages as well.

There was a time, a pitifully short time, indeed, when the fortunes of men were guided by the excellent and wise hands of a Nerva, Trajan, Hadrian, Antoninus Pius and Marcus Aurelius. These few 80 some-odd years saw peace predominate and sagacity upon the throne.

Your coins will have greater meaning if you pursue this magnificent story of a people, without whom there would have been no coins.

Chronological Sketches of the Most Prominent Emperors, Their Families and Contemporaries

Augustus

AUGUSTUS — Gaius (or Caius) Julius Caesar Octavianus. First Roman emperor. Great nephew of Julius Caesar who adopted him as heir to the throne. Joined Mark Antony and Lepidus in forming the Second Triumvirate. Received the title of Augustus from the senate. Ruler of the Roman world in 29 B.C. Died in AD 14 at the age of 77.

LIVIA — Wife of Tiberius Claudius Nero by whom she had two children: Tiberius, later emperor, and Nero Claudius Drusus. Was forced by Augustus to divorce her husband and marry him. Died in AD 29 at the probable age of 85.

Livia

AGRIPPA — Marcus Vipsanius Agrippa. Roman general. A close friend of Augustus and his heir. Predeceased the emperor, however, in 12 BC at the age of 51.

Agrippa

JULIA — Daughter of Augustus. Born 39 BC. Her profligacies forced her father to banish her. She was the wife of the following: Marcellus, Agrippa and the emperor Tiberius. Died in AD 14 at the age of 53.

Julia

CAIUS AND LUCIUS CAESARS — Sons of Agrippa and Julia. Caius died AD 4, Lucius, AD 2.

Caius and Lucius Caesars

TIBERIUS — Tiberius Claudius Nero. The 2nd Roman emperor. Reigned during the time of Christ. Was a just and kind ruler at first, (he became emperor at the death of Augustus who adopted him after the death of Agrippa) but allegedly became base and cruel. Much of this due to the evil influence of Sejanus, Prefect of the Praetorian Guard. He was born in 42 BC, became emperor in AD 14 and died at Capri, where he spent the last 10 years of his life, in the year of AD 37.

Tiberius

DRUSUS, JR. — Born 14 or 15 BC, died AD 23. Son of emperor Tiberius and Vipsania. His wife Livilla was seduced by Sejanus and these two successfully plotted the death, by poisoning, of Drusus.

Drusus, Jr.

NERO CLAUDIUS DRUSUS — Brother of Tiberius and father of emperor Claudius. Died in 9 BC reputedly as a result of being thrown by his horse.

Nero Claudius Drusus

ANTONIA — Daughter of Marc Antony and Octavia. Grandmother of the emperor Nero. She was about 77 years of age at her death.

Antonia

Germanicus

GERMANICUS — Son of Nero Claudius Drusus. Nephew of the emperor Tiberius. A great popular favorite. Died near Antioch in AD 19 possibly by poisoning under orders from Tiberius.

Agrippina the Elder

AGRIPPINA THE ELDER — Daughter of Agrippa and Julia (daughter of Augustus), wife of Germanicus and mother of the emperor Caligula. After the death of her husband she was banished to the island of Pandataria where she died in AD 33 at the probable age of 46.

Nero and Drusus Caesars

NERO AND DRUSUS CAESARS — Sons of Germanicus and Agrippina. Nero died in AD 31, Drusus in AD 33.

Caligula

CALIGULA — Caius Caesar. Roman emperor AD 37-41. Youngest son of Germanicus and Agrippina. From his association with the soldiers in his youth when he wore the Roman boots called caligae, he was named Caligula (little boot). As heir to Tiberius, he ruled with reasonableness at first, but soon became excessively depraved and cruel. He was undoubtedly insane and even thought to name his horse Consul. He was assassinated by the Praetorian guard in AD 41, at the age of 29.

CAESONIA — Fourth wife of Caligula. Murdered with her husband.

Caesonia

DRUSILLA — Sister of Caligula. Daughter of Germanicus and Agrippina.

Drusilla

CLAUDIUS — Tiberius Claudius Drusus. Roman emperor AD 41-54. Son of Nero Claudius Drusus and Antonia. Became emperor by acclamation of the legions upon the death of Caligula. Married four times, his most prominent wives being Messalina, and his niece, the younger Agrippina, who was the mother of the future emperor Nero. She had Claudius adopt her son Nero to the disadvantage of his own son, Britannicus. Her cruelty reached the highest extreme when she had Claudius poisoned in the year AD 54. He was 64 years of age.

Claudius

AGRIPPINA THE YOUNGER — She was the mother of an emperor (Nero), the sister of an emperor (Caligula), daughter of Germanicus and Agrippina. Noted for her excessive cruelties, she was the vicious daughter of a noble and fine mother. After poisoning her husband, the emperor Claudius, she, in turn, was assassinated by agents of her own son Nero in AD 59. She was 44.

Agrippina the Younger

Britannicus

BRITANNICUS—Tiberius Claudius Britannicus. Son of Claudius and Messalina. Having been set aside as the logical heir to the throne due to the intercession of Agrippina Junior on behalf of her own son Nero, he was subsequently poisoned by Nero in AD 55 at the age of 13 or 14.

Nero

NERO — Nero Claudius Caesar Drusus Germanicus. Roman emperor AD 54-68. The first part of Nero's reign was uneventful. What happened thereafter is history which seems to be known by most schoolchildren. He became a terror to the noble families of Rome; poisoned Britannicus, his predecessor's son, poisoned his own mother and even his famous tutor, the philosopher Seneca. He was accused of setting the great fire at Rome and persecuted the Christians because he needed scapegoats for this act. He was finally forced to commit suicide in AD 68 at the age of 31.

Poppaea

POPPAEA — Poppaea Sabina. She was the wife of Crispinus and the mistress of Otho. She subsequently divorced Crispinus to marry Otho. Upon this auspicious occasion she became the mistress of the emperor Nero, so she divorced Otho and married Nero. Her ultimate reward was a violent kick by Nero which resulted in her death, probably in AD 65.

Clodius Macer

CLODIUS MACER — Lucius Clodius Macer. He was propraetor in Africa during the reign of Nero. Refused to recognize Galba as the new emperor after Nero's death and, as a result, was captured by Galba's troops and killed.

GALBA — Roman emperor for 7 months AD 68-69. Proclaimed emperor by the praetorian guard after Nero's suicide. His harsh discipline was resented by his soldiers and he was killed by them. He was 63 years of age.

Galba

OTHO — Marcus Salvius Otho. Emperor for three months in the year AD 69. Envious because he was not named Galba's heir, he led an insurrection and after the death of Galba was proclaimed emperor. He was defeated in battle by Vitellius and committed suicide at the age of 37.

Otho

VITELLIUS — Aulus Vitellius. Emperor, Jan. to Dec., AD 69. His legions proclaimed for him after the death of Galba at the same time Otho's legions declared for Otho. Defeated Otho in battle and was sole emperor for the brief time stated above. The Illyrian legions, meanwhile, declared for Vespasian. Vespasian's forces defeated Vitellius who suffered an ignominious death, afterwards being dragged through the streets by the mob. His banquets, at which he gorged himself, were known far and wide and it was said that if he had paid more attention to affairs of state than to his exploits in eating, he might have survived.

Vitellius

VESPASIAN — Titus Flavius Sabinus Vespasianus. The first of the Flavian emperors. Ruled AD 69-79. Held various offices and became proconsul in Africa under Nero. His legions declared for him while other legions declared for Otho or Vitellius. After Otho's death Vitellius was disposed of and Vespasian assumed the complete power. He was a competent emperor. He died in AD 79 at the age of 70.

Vespasian

Domitilla

DOMITILLA — First wife of Vespasian. Died before he became emperor. She was the mother of the future emperors Titus and Domitian.

Titus

TITUS — Emperor, AD 79-81. Son of Vespasian and Domitilla. Known for his subjection of Judaea in the year 70. He led a rather profligate life before becoming emperor, but upon ascending the throne became an efficient emperor. He died in AD 81 at the age of 41.

Julia Titi

JULIA TITI — Daughter of Titus. Lived for a time with her uncle Domitian as his wife.

Domitian

DOMITIAN — Titus Flavius Domitianus Second son of Vespasian. Emperor AD 81-96. The early part of his reign was uneventful, the latter part found him to be insatiably cruel and tyrannical. He was finally murdered, to the obvious relief of all concerned. His wife Domitia was one of the conspirators. He was 45 at his death.

Nerva

NERVA — Marcus Cocceius Nerva. Emperor AD 96-98. Held responsible offices under Vespasian, Titus and Domitian. Was consul with Domitian in the year AD 90. He was the first of the excellent emperors who were to rule for the next eighty some odd years. He died in AD 98 at the age of 66.

TRAJAN — Marcus Ulpius Trajanus. Emperor AD 98-117. Adopted as Nerva's heir in AD 97. Under him the Roman Empire reached its greatest geographical extent. He was an excellent emperor. He was 65 at his death in AD 117.

Trajan

PLOTINA — Wife of Trajan.

Plotina

MARCIANA — Sister of Trajan.

Marciana

MATIDIA — Daughter of Marciana, mother-in-law of Hadrian.

Matidia

HADRIAN — Publius Aelius Hadrianus. Emperor AD 117-138. Nephew of Trajan and his heir. Erected many fine buildings in Rome and elsewhere. He continued the fine government of his two predecessors. Died in AD 138 at the age of 62.

Hadrian

Sabina

SABINA — Wife of Hadrian. Predeceased him in AD 137.

Aelius

AELIUS — Lucius Aelius Verus Caesar. Adopted by Hadrian as his heir, but he died in AD 138.

Antoninus Pius

ANTONINUS PIUS — Titus Aelius Hadrianus Antoninus. (Originally, before his adoption by Hadrian after the death of Aelius, his name was Titus Aurelius Fulvus Boionius Arrius.) Emperor AD 138-161. Enjoyed a peaceful and prosperous reign. Because of this, history has little to record of his rule. He adopted his nephew Marcus Aurelius whom his daughter Faustina had married.

Faustina the Elder

FAUSTINA THE ELDER — Wife of Antoninus Pius. Her full name was Annia Galeria Faustina. Some writers have said that she was noted for her lack of morals. She died in AD 141 at the age of 37.

MARCUS AURELIUS — Marcus Aelius Aurelius Verus. Emperor, AD 161-180. Had been adopted by Antoninus Pius as his heir, along with Lucius Verus. Verus was his colleague in government. He was a philosopher and was a step towards the Platonic concept of the philosopher king. His "Meditations" are still extant. He was 69 at his death in AD 180.

Marcus Aurelius

ANNIUS VERUS — Son of Marcus Aurelius.

Annius Verus

FAUSTINA THE YOUNGER — Wife of Marcus Aurelius, allegedly noted for her lack of morals, although some scholars question this. She died in AD 175 at the probable age of 50.

Faustina the Younger

LUCIUS VERUS — Lucius Aurelius Verus. Originally Lucius Ceionius Commodus. Colleague of Marcus Aurelius. Had been adopted by Antoninus Pius as had been Marcus Aurelius. Died in AD 169 at the age of 39.

Lucius Verus

LUCILLA — Wife of Lucius Verus and sister of Commodus who, when he became emperor, had her murdered in AD 183.

Lucilla

Commodus

COMMODUS — Lucius Aelius Aurelius Commodus. The abrupt halt to a happy era. The dissolute son of a noble father, he was emperor from AD 180-192. His reign was a retrogression to all of the evil which existed before Nerva. Cruel, intemperate and prodigal, he was finally strangled to death while in a drunken stupor. He was 31 years of age at his death.

Crispina

CRISPINA — Wife of Commodus. He had her killed.

Pertinax

PERTINAX — Publius Helvius Pertinax. Emperor in year AD 193. He was chosen emperor against his will after the death of Commodus. Certain reforms instituted by him met with disfavor and the reactionary element of the praetorian guard murdered him in AD 193.

Didius Julianus

DIDIUS JULIANUS — Marcus Didius Salvius Julianus (or Severus Julianus). Ruled about three months in the year AD 193. The most notable thing about this emperor was the fact that he purchased the throne at auction, an indication of how low the tides of empire had fallen. He was almost immediately unpopular and was slain.

Manlia Scantilla

MANLIA SCANTILLA — Wife of Didius Julianus.

DIDIA CLARA — Daughter of Didius Julianus.

Didia Clara

PESCENNIUS NIGER — Caius Pescennius Niger. Proclaimed emperor by the Syrian legions. The armies of Severus defeated him and he fled only to be subsequently captured and put to death along with all the members of his family in AD 194.

Pescennius Niger

CLODIUS ALBINUS — Decimus Clodius Ceionius Septimius Albinus. Elevated to Caesar under Severus, but after Severus defeated Niger he had the senate declare Albinus a public enemy. After a battle near Lyons, Albinus was defeated and slain in AD 197.

Clodius Albinus

SEPTIMIUS SEVERUS — Lucius Septimius Severus. Emperor, AD 193-211. Held important posts under Marcus Aurelius. Declared against Julianus and Niger as well as Albinus and assumed the supreme control. He was 65 at his death in AD 211.

Septimius Severus

JULIA DOMNA — Wife of the emperor Severus, mother of the emperors Caracalla and Geta. Was a person of considerable intellect. She committed suicide after the death of Caracalla, in AD 217. She was about 50 at her death.

Julia Domna

Caracalla

CARACALLA — Marcus Aurelius Antoninus. Original name, Bassianus. Emperor 211-217. Son of the emperor Severus. Caracalla was a nickname given to him because of the long coat known by that name which he introduced to Rome from Gaul. He was, at first, joint emperor with his brother Geta, but he convinced the praetorian guard to name him sole emperor. He had his brother murdered and, according to some sources, some twenty thousand others as well. He was a treacherous, worthless profligate who was finally murdered by Macrinus. He was 29 years of age at his death in AD 217.

Plautilla

PLAUTILLA — Wife of Caracalla.

Geta

GETA — Lucius Septimius Geta. Younger son of Severus. Joint ruler with his brother Caracalla (209-212). However, the desire on the part of Caracalla for supreme and sole power caused him to have Geta murdered, and effigies, coins, and other permanent works with the image of Geta destroyed. Geta was 23 years of age when he was murdered.

Macrinus

MACRINUS — Marcus Opelius Severus Macrinus Emperor 217-218. Instrumental in the death of Caracalla. The Parthians, in revolt, defeated him. He became unpopular with the army and was subsequently slain in 218 at the age of 54.

DIADUMENIAN — Marcus Opelius Antoninus Diadumenianus. Son of Macrinus. Killed in the revolt which resulted in his father's death.

Diadumenian

ELAGABALUS (HELIOGABALUS) — Marcus Aurelius Antoninus. Originally, Varius Avitus Bassianus. Emperor AD 218-222. He was a priest in the temple of the sun-god (thus his name, Helio-Sun) at Emesa. Defeated Macrinus in battle and then went on to practice extreme debaucheries and cruelties. He was slain by the praetorian guard at the age of 18, dragged along the streets with his mother who also had been slain, and thrown unceremoniously into the Tiber.

Elagabalus

JULIA PAULA — First wife of Elagabalus. He divorced her after a year of marriage.

Julia Paula

AQUILIA SEVERA — Second wife of Elagabalus. He divorced her, but returned to her after divorcing his third wife, Annia Faustina.

Aquilia Severa

ANNIA FAUSTINA — Third wife of Elagabalus. Divorced her and returned to his second wife, Aquilia Severa.

Annia Faustina

Julia Soaemias

JULIA SOAEMIAS — Mother of Elagabalus. Murdered with him in 222.

Julia Maesa

JULIA MAESA — Grandmother of Elagabalus.

Severus Alexander

SEVERUS ALEXANDER — Marcus Aurelius Severus Alexander. Adopted by his cousin Elagabalus as his heir. Ruled from 222-235. He was a just and wise ruler, but was slain by some mutinous soldiers on his way to Germany to subdue a revolt. His mother was slain with him. He was probably 27 years of age at his death.

Orbiana

ORBIANA — Third wife of Severus Alexander.

JULIA MAMAEA — Mother of Severus Alexander. Murdered by mutinous soldiers along with her son in 235.

Julia Mamaea

URANIUS ANTONINUS — Lucius Julius Aurelius Sulpicius Uranius Antoninus. A usurper (235).

Uranius Antoninus

MAXIMINUS I — Caius Julius Verus Maximinus. Had the surname, The Thracian. Emperor 235-238. Was supposed to have been of great size and strength. Was declared emperor by the legions of the Rhine after the death of Severus Alexander. He was cruel and tyrannical and was slain by his own soldiers.

Maximinus I

MAXIMUS — Son of Maximinus I. Murdered with his father in 238.

Maximus

PAULINA — Wife of Maximinus I.

Paulina

GORDIAN AFRICANUS I — Marcus Antonius Gordianus I. Ruled 36 days in the year 238. Was proconsul in Africa under Severus Alexander. Was proclaimed emperor by his followers in Africa and was confirmed by the senate when Maximinus was declared to be a public enemy by that same body. He committed suicide when he learned of the death of his son in battle with one of the supporters of Maximinus.

Gordian Africanus I

Gordian Africanus II

GORDIAN AFRICANUS II — Marcus Antonianus Gordianus II. Son of Gordian I. Associated with his father as co-emperor. Killed in battle at Carthage by Capellianus, the governor of Numidia.

Balbinus

BALBINUS — Decimus Caelius Balbinus. Emperor for about two months in the year 238. He was proclaimed joint emperor by the senate along with Pupienus Maximus, essentially to oppose Maximinus who was threatening Rome. Maximinus was slain, however, and Balbinus was murdered by the Praetorian guard.

Pupienus

PUPIENUS — Marcus Clodius Pupienus Maximus. Appointed joint emperor with Balbinus to oppose Maximinus who threatened Rome. Pupienus was slain by the Praetorian guard, along with Balbinus, after a reign of about two months.

Gordian III (Pius)

GORDIAN III (PIUS) — Marcus Antonius Gordianus. He was the grandson of Gordian I. Proclaimed Caesar during the reign of Balbinus and Pupienus. At their deaths proclaimed emperor by the Praetorian guard at the age of 14 or 15. He ruled for six years (238-244) and through the manipulations of Philip, an officer of the guard, he was murdered at the age of 21. Philip I succeeded him to the throne.

TRANQUILLINA — Wife of Gordian III.

Tranquillina

PHILIP I — Marcus Julius Philippus. An officer of the Praetorian guard during the reign of Gordian Pius. As a result of his machinations, Gordian was slain. Philip was himself killed battling the legions of Trajan Decius. He was emperor from 244-249.

Philip I

OTACILIA SEVERA — Marcia Otacilia Severa. Wife of Philip I.

Otacilia Severa

PHILIP II — Marcus Julius Severus Philippus. Son of Philip I. Was murdered soon after his father.

Philip II

PACATIAN — A usurper about whom very little is known (c.AD 248).

JOTAPIAN — A Syrian usurper about whom little is known (c.AD 248).

Jotapian

Trajan Decius

TRAJAN DECIUS — Caius Messius Quintus Traianus Decius. Emperor 249-251. Was commander of the troops of Danube during the reign of Philip I. His soldiers revolted against Philip and he was forced to become emperor by them against his will. He defeated Philip in battle and Philip was killed. Decius was slain in Thrace battling the Goths. He was 53 years of age at his death.

Etruscilla

ETRUSCILLA — Wife of Trajan Decius.

Herennius Etruscus

HERENNIUS ETRUSCUS — Quintus Herennius Etruscus Messius Decius. Son of Trajan Decius and killed at the same time as his father.

Hostilian

HOSTILIAN — Caius Valens Hostilianus Messius Quintus. A younger son of Trajan Decius about whom little is known.

Trebonianus Gallus

TREBONIANUS GALLUS — Caius Vibius Trebonianus Gallus. Emperor 251-254. Appointed to serve as Hostilian's associate. He effected a peace with the Goths which was felt to be degrading by the Romans. He was subsequently murdered by his own soldiers.

VOLUSIAN — Caius Vibius Volusianus Trebonianus Asinius. Son of Trebonianus Gallus. Killed at the same time as his father.

Volusian

AEMILIAN — Marcus Aemilius Aemilianus. (253-254). A governor of Pannonia and Moesia during the reign of Gallus. He was hailed as emperor by his troops and defeated the forces of Gallus in battle. He was murdered by his own soldiers.

Aemilian

CORNELIA SUPERA — Wife of Aemilian.

Cornelia Supera

VALERIAN — Publius Licinius Valerianus. Emperor 253-260. Of noble birth, he was loyal to Gallus but could give him no help in his battle with Aemilian, arriving too late. At the death of Gallus was proclaimed emperor and associated his son Gallienus with him. Troubles on the borders forced him into many battles. Was defeated by the Persian, Shapuri, and held captive until his death.

Valerian

Mariniana

MARINIANA — Wife of Valerian.

Gallienus

GALLIENUS — Publius Licinius Valerianus Egnatius Gallienus. Son of Valerian. Emperor 253-268. Became sole emperor after the capture of his father by the Persians. He was obliged to deal with disintegration from within the empire and from without. It proved to be too great a task. He was killed by his own soldiers at the age of 50.

Saloninus

SALONINUS — Son of Gallienus. Killed by Postumus in AD 259.

Salonina

SALONINA — Wife of Gallienus.

Valerian II

VALERIAN II — Son of Gallienus. Died about 255.

MACRIANUS I — Marcus Fulvius Macrianus. (260-261). It was due to his incompetence that the Roman army of Valerian was defeated, resulting in the capture of the emperor. Nevertheless, Macrianus was declared emperor by his troops. On his way back to Italy he was met in battle by one of Valerian's generals and was defeated and slain.

Macrianus I

MACRIANUS II — Titus Fulvius Julius Macrianus. (260-261). Son of Macrianus. Slain at the same time as his father.

Macrianus II

QUIETUS — Fulvius Julius Quietus. (260-261). Youngest son of Macrianus I. When his father left for Rome after the Eastern campaign, he was left to administer affairs. He was attacked by the king of the Palmyrans, defeated, captured and killed.

Quietus

REGALIANUS — Publius Caius Regalianus. (260-261). A general under Valerian. At Valerian's death, he seized the power in Pannonia but was killed shortly thereafter.

Regalianus

DRYANTILLA — Wife of Regalianus.

POSTUMUS — Marcus Cassianus Latinus Postumus. Emperor 259-267. Governor of Gaul under Valerian. After declaring himself emperor, during the reign of Valerian, he ruled in Britain and in Gaul. He was a wise ruler but was killed in battle as a result of his usurpations.

Postumus

Laelianus

LAELIANUS — Ulpius Cornelius Laelianus (267). Led a revolt against Postumus and was killed.

Victorinus

VICTORINUS — Marcus Piavvonius Victorinus. (265-270?) Sole ruler of Gaul after having been co-emperor with Postumus. Assassinated by his own soldiers.

Marius

MARIUS — Caius Marcus Aurelius Marius (268). Proclaimed himself emperor at the death of Postumus, but was killed almost immediately, probably within a few days.

Tetricus I

TETRICUS I — C Pius Esuvius Tetricus. (267-276) Declared himself emperor and associated his son with him. He finally abdicated and, strange as it seems, was allowed to live out his days in Rome.

Tetricus II

TETRICUS II — Caius Pius Esuvius Tetricus. (272-276). Son of Tetricus the Elder and associated with his father in his father's rule. He was spared death upon the abdication of his father and himself after being defeated by Aurelian at Chalons.

*Claudius II
Gothicus*

CLAUDIUS II-GOTHICUS — Marcus Aurelius Claudius. Emperor 268-270. Possessed an excellent military record under Decius, Valerian and Gallienus. Fought two great battles; against the Alamanni in northern Italy and the Goths in Moesia from which he obtained the title "Gothicus." He died during a plague in the year 270 at the age of 56.

QUINTILLUS — Caius Marcus Aurelius Claudius Quintillus. Emperor 270. Supported as emperor at the death of Claudius, but the legions of Sirmium declared for Aurelian. He ultimately committed suicide.

Quintillus

AURELIAN — Lucius Domitius Aurelianus. Emperor 270-275. Known as Restitutor Orbis (Restorer of the Empire). Occupied high military positions under Valerian and Claudius II. Pushed Goths across the Danube. Defeated Palmyra and brought the queen, Zenobia, back to Rome. Reconquered Egypt and fortified Rome. He was murdered as a result of a conspiracy at the age of 63.

Aurelian

SEVERINA — Wife of Aurelian.

Severina

VABALATHUS — Son of Zenobia, queen of Palmyra. Ruler of that state under his mother's tutelage.

Vabalathus

ZENOBIA — Queen of Palmyra. Captured by Aurelian and brought to Rome. She was eventually pardoned and allowed to live in Italy.

Zenobia

Tacitus

TACITUS — Marcus Claudius Tacitus. Emperor 275-276. Elected by the senate after the death of Aurelian. Claimed descent from the famous historian. Ruled for about six months. Was killed by his soldiers at the age of 76.

Florianus

FLORIANUS — Marcus Annius Florianus. Emperor for a few weeks in 276. Seized power at the death of his half brother Tacitus. Opposed by Probus and killed in battle.

Probus

PROBUS — Marcus Aurelius Probus. Emperor 276-282. Was governor of the east under Tacitus after serving in a distinguished manner in the armies of Valerian, Claudius and Aurelian. Initiated many beneficial improvements in government, but he was killed by mutinous soldiers.

Carus

CARUS — Marcus Aurelius Carus. Emperor 282-283. Prefect of the praetorian guard under Probus. At the death of Probus chosen emperor by the soldiers. Appointed his sons Carinus and Numerian as Caesars. While fighting the Persians he was killed, either in battle, or, according to some versions, struck by lightning.

CARINUS — Marcus Aurelius Carinus. Emperor 283-285. Eldest son of Carus. Appointed governor of the western provinces while his father and brother Numerian proceeded against the Persians. Defeated Diocletian in battle, but was murdered by one of his own officers.

Carinus

MAGNIA URBICA — Wife of Carinus.

Magnia Urbica

NIGRINIAN — Possibly a son of Carinus.

Nigrinian

NUMERIAN — Marcus Aurelius Numerianus. Emperor 283-284, jointly with his brother Carinus. He died shortly after his father, Carus.

Numerian

JULIAN — Marcus Aurelius Julianus. A rebellious general who served under the emperor Carinus. He was slain in 285.

Julian

Diocletian

DIOCLETIAN — Caius Aurelius Valerius Diocletianus. Emperor 284-305. Born at Dioclea in Dalmatia from where his name was derived. Held commands under Probus, Aurelian and Carus. Was proclaimed emperor at the death of Numerian. Was associated with Maximianus I, and later with Galerius and Constantius Chlorus Viciously persecuted the Christians, but on the other hand, he did much to reform the internal affairs of the empire. He abdicated in 305 and lived out his life in retirement. He was 68 at his death.

Maximian I (Herculius)

MAXIMIAN I (HERCULIUS) — Marcus Aurelius Valerius Maximianus. Emperor 286-305. Born in Pannonia of humble origin. Was associated with the emperor Diocletian. He abdicated with Diocletian (305) but returned to champion the cause of his son, Maxentius, who had claimed the throne in opposition to Galerius and Constantius. Because of complicity in a plot against Constantine, he was ordered to end his own life.

Carausius

CARAUSIUS — Marcus Aurelius Mausaeus Carausius. Usurper in Britain (287-293). Was in command of the fleet in northern Gaul, but taking advantage of his position, he turned to indiscriminate plunder and fell into disfavor. Fled to Britain and proclaimed himself emperor. He was defeated by the fleet of Maximian and was slain by his chief minister Allectus. He was probably 48 years old at his death.

Allectus

ALLECTUS — Caius Allectus. The chief minister of Carausius, he was the cause of the latter's death. Declared himself emperor and ruled cruelly (293-296). The legions of Constantius killed him in a battle in Britain.

CONSTANTIUS I (CHLORUS) — Flavius Valerius Constantius. Caesar 295-305; Augustus 305-306. Son-in-law of Maximian, father of Constantine the Great. Adopted as Caesar by Maximian. Upon abdication of Diocletian and Maximian assumed full power. He died in 306 at the age of 56.

Constantius I (Chlorus)

HELENA — Wife of Constantius I. Mother of Constantine the Great.

Helena

GALERIUS — Caius Galerius Valerius Maximianus. Caesar, 293-305; Augustus, 305-311. Created Caesar by Diocletian. Was beaten by the Persians, but subsequently inflicted a great defeat upon them. Extremely inimical to the Christians and probably had much to do with persuading Diocletian to persecute them. As emperor he elevated Licinius to the rank of Caesar. He died in 311.

Galerius

GALERIA VALERIA — Daughter of Diocletian; second wife of Galerius.

Galeria Valeria

SEVERUS II — Flavius Valerius Severus. Caesar, 305-306; Augustus, 306-307. Created Caesar by Galerius who also named him Augustus. He was unsuccessful in battle with Maxentius and was forced to commit suicide.

Severus II

Maxentius

MAXENTIUS — Marcus Aurelius Valerius Maxentius. Son of Maximian. Emperor 306-312. Not being a particularly admirable person he was passed over when his father and Diocletian appointed the new Caesars. Led an uprising and was proclaimed Caesar by the praetorian guard. He overthrew Severus and drove Galerius from Italy. Attacked Constantine and suffered a complete defeat. He drowned while fleeing across the Tiber.

ROMULUS — Son of Maxentius.

Romulus

Alexander

ALEXANDER — A usurper in Africa. Governor of that province under Maxentius. Proclaimed himself emperor, but was crushed almost immediately.

Maximinus II (Daza)

MAXIMINUS II (DAZA) — Galerius Valerius Maximinus. Maximinus was a nephew of the emperor Galerius and was made Caesar in 305 at which time he governed Egypt and Syria. Became emperor in 308 and was defeated by Licinius. He died in 314.

Licinius

LICINIUS I — Publius Flavius Galerius Valerius Licianus Licinius. Emperor 307-324. Given the rank of Augustus by Galerius. He married a half-sister of Constantine the Great and with him issued the edict of Milan recognizing Christianity. He and Maximinus Daza agreed to rule jointly. Maximinus, however, attacked him and was defeated. There was not lasting amity between Licinius and Constantine and in making war upon Constantine, Licinius was seized and slain. He was probably 55 years of age at his death.

LICINIUS II — Flavius Valerius Licinius. Son of Licinius I. He was put to death, shortly after his father, at the age of 9.

Licinius II

VALENS — Aurelius Valerius Valens. Created Augustus (314) by Licinius but murdered shortly thereafter.

Valens

MARTINIAN — Marcus Martinianus. Created Augustus by Licinius (323). Seized and put to death with the latter.

Martinian

CONSTANTINE I (THE GREAT) — Flavius Valerius Aurelius Constantinus. Caesar, 306-308; Augustus, 308-337. Son of Constantius Chlorus. At the time he was proclaimed Caesar by his father there were five claimants to the throne. Defeated Maxentius and then Licinius to secure authority. Devoted much time to internal administration, strengthening of the borders, elimination of abuses. By the Edict of Milan he recognized Christianity. Called the Council of Nicaea (325) where the Nicene Creed was adopted Chose Byzantium as the new capital of the empire and renamed it Constantinople. He was probably 57 years of age at his death.

*Constantine I
(The Great)*

THEODORA — Flavia Maxima Theodora. Second wife of Constantius Chlorus.

Fausta

FAUSTA — Flavia Maxima Fausta. Wife of Constantine the Great and daughter of Maximianus Herculius.

Crispus

CRISPUS — Flavius Julius Crispus. Son of Constantine the Great. He was a great popular favorite and this possibly was, in part, the cause of his death, by his father's orders. He was Caesar from 317-326.

Delmatius

DELMATIUS — Flavius Julius Delmatius. Nephew of Constantine the Great. Caesar 335-337. Murdered after the death of Constantine.

Hanniballianus

HANNIBALLIANUS — Flavius Claudius Hanniballianus. Caesar, 335-337. Murdered along with his brother Delmatius. They were nephews of Constantine.

Constantine II

CONSTANTINE II — Flavius Claudius Julius Constantinus. Son of Constantine the Great. Emperor 337-340. Joint emperor with his brothers Constantius and Constans at his father's death. In warring with Constans he was killed.

CONSTANS — Flavius Julius Constans. Caesar, 333-337. Augustus, 337-350. His share of the empire at the death of Constantine the Great consisted of Italy, Africa and Illyricum. In war with his brothers he defeated and killed Constantine II. Later, Magnentius attacked him and Constans was overtaken while fleeing and was killed.

Constans

CONSTANTIUS II — Flavius Julius Constantius. Caesar, 323-337; Augustus, 337-361. Son of Constantine and Fausta. Defeated Magnentius after having become sole ruler at the death of Constans. The empire enjoyed a few years of peace during his reign. However, he learned that his cousin Julian had proclaimed himself emperor and in moving to crush thus unsurper he died at the age of 44.

Constantius II

CONSTANTIUS GALLUS — Flavius Claudius Constantius. A nephew of Constantine the Great, who usurped the power in the east. His rule of oppression brought him to trial and he was executed (354).

Constantius Gallus

NEPOTIAN — Flavius Popilius Nepotianus Constantius. Emperor for a brief time in 350. A nephew of Constantine the Great. He seized the throne of Constans, but was killed almost immediately in a battle with Magnentius.

Nepotian

VETRANIO — Proclaimed emperor by his troops at the death of Constans. After a reign of less than a year (350-351) he retired and lived out his years in peace.

Vetranio

249

Magnentius

MAGNENTIUS — Flavius Popilius Magnentius. Emperor 350-353. Of barbarian birth, he was in command of the troops of the Rhine. Caused the death of Constans and was proclaimed emperor. He was defeated by Constantius II and fled to Gaul where he committed suicide.

Decentius

DECENTIUS — Magnus Decentius. Brother of Magnentius. Upon hearing of the suicide of his brother he, too, committed suicide (353).

Julian II

JULIAN II — Flavius Claudius Julianus. Emperor 361-363. Known as Julian the Apostate. Well educated. He was the brother of Julius Constantius who was a half-brother of Constantine the Great. Proclaimed emperor by his troops in a revolt against the latter. At the death of Constantius he became sole ruler. He was killed during one of his battles with the Persians. He was 32 years of age at his death.

Helena

HELENA — Daughter of Constantine the Great and wife of Julian II.

Jovian

JOVIAN — Flavius Claudius Jovianus. Emperor 363-364. General of army under Julian. Proclaimed emperor by his soldiers after the death of the latter. Made an unhappy peace with the Persians by giving up the provinces beyond the Tigris. Supported the Nicene Creed; restored privileges to the Christians. Died an obscure death in Galatia. He was probably 33 years of age at his death.

VALENTINIAN I — Flavius Valentinianus. Emperor 364-375. Of poor parentage, he entered the army and moved swiftly through the ranks. Held in disfavor by both Constantius and Julian (the latter banished him). At the death of Jovian chosen emperor; appointed Valens, his brother, as associate. His reign knew the encroachments of many barbarian tribes. Died in 375 at the age of 54.

Valentinian I

VALENS — Younger brother of Valentinian I. Made emperor of the east by his brother. Waged war unsuccessfully against the Goths. Made a disgraceful treaty with the Persians. He was subsequently defeated and slain by the Goths. Was emperor from 364-378.

Valens

PROCOPIUS — A usurper who rebelled against Valens. He was executed (366).

Procopius

GRATIAN — Flavius Gratianus. Emperor 375-383. Son of Valentinian I. He and a brother, Valentinian II, were joint Augusti of the west. At the defeat of Valens also became emperor in the east, with Theodosius as his colleague. Killed in battle with Magnus Maximus at the age of 24.

Gratian

VALENTINIAN II — Son of Valentinian I and younger brother of Gratian. Emperor, jointly with his brother (375-383). Emperor until 392. He was 3 years of age when proclaimed emperor, under the guardianship of the Empress Justina. He was murdered by one of his generals, Arbogast, at the age of 20.

Valentinian II

*Theodosius I
(The Great)*

THEODOSIUS I (THE GREAT) — Flavius Theodosius. Emperor 379-395. Summoned to serve as associate by Gratian at the death of Valens. A cruel ruler, he died at Milan, after having made his sons, Honorius and Arcadius, Caesars. He was about 50 at his death.

Aelia Flaccilla

AELIA FLACCILLA — Wife of Theodosius I.

Magnus Maximus

MAGNUS MAXIMUS — Magnus Clemens Maximus. Emperor 383-388. Declared emperor by his soldiers who did not favor Gratian. He defeated Gratian in battle, but subsequently met with Theodosius who had him executed.

Flavius Victor

FLAVIUS VICTOR (387-388) — Son of Magnus Maximus. He was defeated fighting the Franks in Gaul, taken prisoner and executed.

Eugenius

EUGENIUS — Proclaimed emperor after the murder of Valentinian II. Captured and slain by Theodosius (394).

HONORIUS — Flavius Honorius. Emperor of the west, 395-423. Second son of Theodosius the Great. His reign was one of constant turmoil due to attacks by the Visigoths under Alaric. Roman power suffered a severe decline under this inept rule. He was 39 at his death.

Honorius

ARCADIUS — Emperor (395-408.) Son of Theodosius I. Affairs of state did not interest him and the government was ruled by others. Alaric, the Goth, ruled at this time in what is now the Balkan region. Arcadius died in 408 at the age of 31.

Arcadius

CONSTANTIUS III — Emperor 421. Roman general raised to rank of Augustus by Honorius. Reigned only seven months.

Constantius III

GALLA PLACIDIA — Daughter of Theodosius the Great.

Galla Placidia

CONSTANTINE III — Usurper in Gaul and Britain. (407-411).

CONSTANS — Son of Constantine III. (408-411).

Constantine III

Maximus

MAXIMUS — Usurper in Spain. Publicly executed by Honorius. (409-411).

Jovinus

JOVINUS — Usurper in Gaul. Killed by the Goths. (411-413).

SEBASTIANUS (412-413)—Brother of Jovinus. Killed with him.

Priscus Attalus

PRISCUS ATTALUS — Usurper in Gaul. (409-410).

Johannes

JOHANNES — Proclaimed himself emperor after the death of Honorius. Defeated by Theodosius. (423-425).

Valentinian III

VALENTINIAN III — Son of Constantius III. Murdered. (425-455).

PETRONIUS MAXIMUS — Named emperor after the death of Valentinian III. Murdered within a few months. (455).

LICINIA EUDOXIA — Daughter of Theodosius II. Wife of Valentinian III.

Petronius Maximus

AVITUS — Emperor after the death of Petronius, 455-456. Deposed in a little over a year.

Avitus

MAJORIAN — Emperor after Avitus (457-461). Assassinated by one of his generals.

Majorian

SEVERUS III — Emperor after Majorian (461-465). Poisoned by the same general who assassinated Majorian (Ricimer).

Severus III

ANTHEMIUS — A general in the eastern army. Proclaimed emperor by the Roman people, but assassinated by Ricimer. (467-472).

Anthemius

Euphemia

EUPHEMIA — Wife of Anthemius.

OLYBRIUS — Son-in-law of Valentinian III. Sent to Italy to kill Ricimer, but Ricimer made him emperor. He died shortly thereafter. (472.)

Glycerius

GLYCERIUS — Emperor at Ravenna (473-474). Dethroned by Julius Nepos. Died a few years later.

Julius Nepos

JULIUS NEPOS — Emperor of the west after deposing Glycerius. Was deposed in 474 by Orestes, father of Romulus Augustus, the last emperor of the west.

Romulus Augustus

ROMULUS AUGUSTUS — Last emperor of the west (475-476). Son of Orestes, but ruled in name only. Deposed by Odoacer, king of the Herculi. Retired and died at Campania.

The Use of the Inscription in Determining the Year A Coin Was Struck

A careful consideration of certain parts of the inscriptions on the coins of the empire, up until about the beginning of the third century, frequently will reveal the date that particular coin was struck.

The three most prominent means of such a determination are by:

1. The TR P
2. The COS
3. The IMP

It must be remembered, as explained elsewhere in this book, that the tribunician power was granted to the emperor for his lifetime, but that it was renewed annually. When it was so renewed each renewal would be indicated by the placing of a numeral after the TR P. Thus, TR P III would indicate that the coin was struck during the third year the emperor held such a title. Using a more specific example, a coin of the emperor Nerva upon which TR P II was inscribed would first indicate that the coin was struck during the second year he held the title. Using the chart which follows, it would be indicated that his second TR P was in the year 97. As further confirmation, and in order to deal with exceptions to this procedure, we would also examine the dates of his consulship and the dates or years in which he received the title Imperator by acclamation.

COS is the abbreviation of Consul. The emperor, most normally, served as one of the two consuls of the Roman state. Frequently, however, he designated another to serve in his stead. Inasmuch as any and all consulships were for one year only, and, further, inasmuch as the Romans used the same system of using numerals after the COS as they did with the TR P, it is often possible to determine the date of a coin by the COS. The outstanding difficulty in using the COS by itself, however, lies in the aforementioned fact that quite frequently a period of years passed before an emperor would pick up the consulship again. A good example would be indicated in examining the consulships of the emperor Augustus. The chart shows us that he served his COS XI in the year 23 BC and his COS XII in 5 BC. As further demonstration, a coin of the emperor Vespasian bearing the title COS IIII (NOTE: Roman coins show the numeral four written as above, not as IV) could have been struck either in the year 72 or the year 73, for his COS V was not served until 74 and his COS III was served in the year 71. On the other hand, a coin of the emperor Domitian bearing COS X upon it would have had to have been struck in the year 84 because his COS VIIII was served in the year 83 and his COS XI was served in the year 85.

And yet a third means of finding the date of your coin may be found in the IMP part of the inscription. The IMP here referred to is that title which we have called the IMP by acclamation. It should be recalled that the emperor added numbers after this title, also, to designate extraordinary events or victories in the field by his commanders. Thus, in examining a particular coin of the emperor Marcus Aurelius we find, as part of the inscription, the following: TR P XXIX, IMP VII, COS III. Studying the charts we find this information:

1. If his TR P II was in the year 147, his TR P XXIX occurred 27 years later, or in the year 174.

2. His third consulship (COS III) was served in the year 161. Apparently, we have a discrepancy, but careful observation will indicate that no more consulships appear upon the chart. The next step, then, is to turn to the IMP part of the inscription.

3. IMP VII appears in the chart under the year of 174. Our conclusion, then, is that the coin was struck in that year. The above example will indicate why it is necessary to approach the charts from every possible angle before arriving at a conclusion. Occasionally, other titles might prove to be of some help, titles such as P P, CENSOR, or hereditary and honorary titles. However, too much faith should not be placed in the latter because of the generally extensive period covered by these titles.

In conclusion, it is necessary to say a word about the classification of the coins of the later empire, coins upon which practically none of the titles which we have been discussing appear. Such a classification requires knowledge far beyond the scope of this book, for here are involved questions of the subtle variances of style, of texture, of fabric, and other factors, complex and difficult. Quite frequently, the cultural background of the particular time in question must be studied and analyzed. In brief, it is a study in itself, a study which requires years of practice and effort.

The chart with TR P dates begins on page 273.

AUGUSTUS		TIBERIUS
COS XI	23 BC	
IMP VIIII	20 BC	
IMP X	15 BC	
	13 BC	COS
IMP XI	12 BC	
P M		
IMP XII	11 BC	
IMP XIII	9 BC	
IMP XIIII	8 BC	
	7 BC	COS II
COS XII	5 BC	
COS XIII	2 BC	

AUGUSTUS		TIBERIUS
P P		
IMP XV	AD 2	
IMP XVI (?)	AD 6	
IMP XVII	AD 6	IMP III
IMP XVIII		IMP IIII
IMP XIX	AD 9	IMP V
IMP XX	AD 11	IMP VI
	AD 12	IMP VII
IMP XXI	AD 14	PRINCEPS
	AD 15	P M
	AD 18	COS III
		IMP VIII
	AD 21	COS IIII
	AD 31	COS V

CALIGULA		CLAUDIUS
IMP	AD 37	
P M		
COS		
P P	AD 38	
COS II	AD 39	
COS III	AD 40	
COS IIII	AD 41	IMP
		IMP II
		IMP III
		IMP IIII
		P M
	AD 42	COS II
		P P
	AD 43	COS III
	AD 44	IMP V
		IMP VI
		IMP VII
	AD 45	IMP VIII
	AD 46	IMP VIIII
		IMP X
		IMP XI
	AD 47	COS IIII
		IMP XII
		IMP XIII
	AD 48	IMP XIIII
		IMP XV
	AD 48	CENSOR

CALIGULA	CLAUDIUS
	AD 49.........IMP XVI
	AD 50.........IMP XVII
	IMP XVIII
	AD 51.........COS V
	IMP XXI
	AD 52.........IMP XXIIII
	AD 53.........IMP XXVII

NERO	GALBA: OTHO: VITELLIUS
IMP...............................AD 54	
P M	
COS...............................AD 55	
P P	
COS II ....AD 57	
IMP III	
COS III...........................AD 58	
IMP IIII	
IMP V	
IMP VI............................AD 59	
COS IIII ....AD 60	
IMP VII	
IMP VIII..........................AD 61	
IMP VIIII	
IMP XI............................AD 66	
IMP XII ....AD 67	
COS V ....AD 68.........IMP: P M (Galba)
	AD 69.........COS II (Galba)
	AD 69.........IMP: COS: P M (Otho)
	AD 69.........IMP: GERM: COS (Vitellius)

VESPASIAN

IMP...............................AD 69	
IMP II	
COS...............................AD 69	
P M	
P P	
COS II ....AD 70	
IMP III	
IMP IIII	
IMP V	

VESPASIAN

COS III	AD 71
IMP VI	
IMP VII	
IMP VIII	
COS IIII	AD 72
IMP X	AD 73
COS V	AD 74
IMP XI	
IMP XII	
COS VI	AD 75
IMP XIII	
IMP XIIII	
COS VII	AD 76
IMP XV	
IMP XVI	
IMP XVII	
IMP XVIII	
COS VIII	AD 77
IMP XIX	AD 78
COS VIIII	AD 79
IMP XX	
AUG	
P M	

TITUS   DOMITIAN

COS	AD 70	
IMP	AD 71	COS
IMP II		
P M		
COS II	AD 72	
IMP III		
CENSOR	AD 73	COS II
IMP IIII		
COS III	AD 74	COS III
IMP VI		
IMP VII		
COS IIII	AD 75	
IMP VII		
IMP VIII		
COS V	AD 76	COS IIII
IMP VIIII (?)		
IMP X (?)		
IMP XI		

TITUS		DOMITIAN
IMP XII		
COS VI	AD 77	COS V
IMP XIII	AD 78	
COS VII	AD 79	COS VI
IMP XIIII		
IMP XV		
AUG		
P M		
P P		
COS VIII	AD 80	COS VII
IMP XVI	AD 81	IMP
IMP XVII		AUG
		P M
		P P
	AD 82	COS VIII
		IMP II
	AD 83	COS VIIII
		IMP III
		IMP IIII (?)
	AD 84	COS X
		IMP V
		IMP VI

DOMITIAN		NERVA
IMP VII	AD 84	
GERM		
COS XI	AD 85	
IMP VIII		
IMP VIIII		
IMP X		
IMP XI		
CENS PERPET		
COS XII	AD 86	
IMP XII		
IMP XIII		
IMP XIIII		
COS XIII	AD 87	
COS XIIII	AD 88	
IMP XV		
IMP XVI		
IMP XVII		
IMP XVIII		
IMP XIX		

DOMITIAN	NERVA
IMP XX	
IMP XXI	
COS XV ....AD 90	
COS XVI.................................AD 92	
COS XVII...............................AD 95	
	AD 96.........COS II
	IMP
	CAES
	AUG
	AD 97.........COS II
	IMP II
	GERM
	AD 98.........COS IIII

TRAJAN	HADRIAN
CAES ....AD 97	
IMP	
GERM ....AD 97	
COS II ....AD 98	
AUG	
P M	
P P	
COS III...................................AD 100	
COS IIII ....AD 101	
IMP II	
IMP III ....AD 102	
IMP IIII	
COS V ....AD 103	
IMP V.....................................AD 105	
IMP VI ....AD 106	
COS VI....................................AD 112	
OPTIMUS................................AD 114	
IMP VIII.................................AD 115	
IMP VIIII	
IMP X	
IMP XI	
IMP XII	
IMP XIII (?)	
PARTHICUS.............................AD 116	
	AD 117.......COS
	IMP
	CAES
	AUG

TRAJAN	HADRIAN
	P M
	P P
AD 118.......COS II
AD 119.......COS III
AD 128.......P P
AD 135.......IMP II

AELIUS

COS..AD 136	
CAES	
P M...AD 136	
COS II..AD 137	
	AD 138.......COS
	CAES
	IMP
	AUG
	P M
	PIUS
	COS DES II
	AD 139.......COS II
	COS DES III
	IMP II
	P P
	AD 140.......COS III
	AD 144.......COS DES IIII
	AD 145.......COS IIII

MARCUS AURELIUS   LUCIUS VERUS

MARCUS AURELIUS	LUCIUS VERUS
CAES ....AD 139	
COS DES	
COS...AD 140	
COS DES II...................................AD 144	
COS II ....AD 145	
P M...AD 147.......CAES
	AD 154.......COS
COS III...AD 161.......COS II
IMP	IMP
AUG	AUG
	P M
IMP II..AD 163.......IMP II:
	ARMENIACUS

MARCUS AURELIUS		LUCIUS VERUS
ARMENIACUS	AD 164	
IMP III	AD 165	IMP III: PARTHICUS
MEDICUS	AD 166	MEDICUS
PARTHICUS		IMP IIII
IMP IIII		
P P	AD 167	COS III
		P P
IMP V	AD 168	IMP V
IMP VI	AD 171	
GERM	AD 172	
IMP VII	AD 174	
SARMATICUS	AD 175	
IMP VIII		
IMP VIIII	AD 177	
IMP X	AD 179	

COMMODUS

CAES	AD 166
GERM	AD 172
SARMATICUS	AD 175
IMP	AD 176
COS	AD 177
IMP II	
AUG	
P P	
IMP III	AD 179
COS II	
IMP IIII	AD 180
COS III	AD 181
IMP V	AD 182
COS IIII	AD 183
IMP VI	
PIUS	
P M	
IMP VII	AD 184
BRITANNICUS	
FELIX	AD 185
COS V	AD 186
IMP VIII	
COS VI	AD 190

COMMODUS	PERTINAX: DIDIUS JULIANUS: CLODIUS ALBINUS:
COS VII ....AD 192.......COS II (Pertinax)	
AD 193.......IMP: AUG: P M: P P (Pertinax)	
AD 193.......IMP: CAES: AUG (Didius)	
AD 193.......COS: (Clodius)	
AD 194.......COS II (Clodius)	

SEPTIMIUS SEVERUS	CARACALLA
COS...............................AD 193	
IMP	
CAES	
AUG	
P M	
P P	
COS II ....AD 194	
IMP II	
IMP III	
IMP IIII	
PIUS ....AD 195	
PARTHICUS	
ARABICUS	
ADIABENICUS	
IMP V	
IMP VI	
IMP VII	
IMP VIII...........................AD 196.......CAES	
IMP VIIII ....AD 197.......P M	
IMP X	
IMP XI.............................AD 198.......IMP	
AUG	
AD 201 ......PIUS	
FELIX	
PARTHICUS	
COS III...........................AD 202.......COS	
AD 205 ......COS II	
AD 207 ......IMP II	
AD 208 ......COS III	
P P	
BRITANNICUS.........................AD 209	

SEPTIMIUS SEVERUS	CARACALLA
IMP XV	
	AD 210 ......BRITANNICUS
	AD 211 ......P M

CARACALLA	GETA
	AD 198 ......CAES
	AD 205 ......COS
	AD 208 ......COS II
	AD 209 ......AUG
	PIUS
	AD 210 ......BRITANNICUS
	AD 211 ......IMP
	P P
COS IIII ....AD 213	
GERM	
IMP III	
INVICTUS	
IMP IIII ....AD 214	

MACRINUS: DIADUMENIAN	ELAGABALUS
IMP: CAES: AUG: P M:	
P P (Macrinus) ....AD 217	
CAES (Diadumenian) ....AD 217	
COS II (Macrinus) ....AD 218 ....IMP	
IMP: AUG (Diadumenian)	CAES
	COS
	AUG
	P M
	P P
	AD 219 ....COS II
	AD 220 ....COS III
	AD 222 ....COS IIII

SEVERUS ALEXANDER	MAXIMINUS
CAES ....AD 221	
P M	
COS...AD 222	
IMP	

SEVERUS ALEXANDER | MAXIMINUS

SEVERUS ALEXANDER		MAXIMINUS
AUG		
P P		
COS II	AD 226	
COS III	AD 229	
	AD 235	IMP
		CAES
		AUG
		P M
		P P
	AD 236	GERM
		IMP III
		IMP IIII
	AD 237	IMP V
		IMP VI
	AD 238	IMP VII

GORDIAN I / GORDIAN II | BALBINUS

GORDIAN I GORDIAN II		BALBINUS
IMP: CAES: AUG: P M		
P P (Gordian I)	AD 238	IMP: CAES: AUG: P M
IMP: CAES: AUG: P M		
(Gordian II)	AD 238	

PUPIENUS | GORDIAN III

PUPIENUS		GORDIAN III
CAES	AD 235	
GERM	AD 238	CAES
SARMATICUS		AUG
DACICUS		IMP
IMP	AD 238	P M
AUG		P P
P M		
P P		
	AD 239	COS
	AD 240	IMP II
		IMP III
	AD 241	COS II
	AD 242	IMP VI

PHILIP I	PHILIP II
IMP ....AD 244............	NOB C
CAES	
AUG	
P P	
P M	
PARTHICUS	
PERSICUS	
COS ....AD 245	
AD 246...........	AUG
COS II............................AD 247...........	IMP
	CAES
	AUG
	P M
	P P
COS III ....AD 248...........	COS II
CARPICUS	CARPICUS
GERM	GERM

TRAJAN DECIUS:
HERENNIUS ETRUSCUS:
HOSTILIAN

IMP: CAES: AUG: P M: AD 249
P P (Decius)
COS II (Decius) ....AD 250
CAES (Herennius)...............AD 250
CAES Hostilian ....AD 250

TRAJAN DECIUS:	TREBONIANUS GALLUS:
HERENNIUS ETRUSCUS:	VOLUSIAN:
HOSTILIAN	AEMILIAN
AUG (Hostilian).................AD 250	
COS III (Decius)................AD 251	
DACICUS (Decius)	
COS: AUG (Herennius) .....AD 251...........	IMP: CAES: AUG:
	P M: P P (Trebonianus)
AD 251...........	CAES: AUG: P M:
	P P: (Volusian)
AD 252	COS II (Trebonianus)
AD 252	COS (Volusian)
AD 253	COS II (Volusian)
AD 253	IMP: CAES: AUG:
	(Aemilian)

VALERIAN		GALLIENUS
IMP	AD 253	IMP
CAES		CAES
AUG		AUG
P M		P M
P P		P P
COS		
COS II	AD 254	COS
IMP VII		
COS III	AD 255	COS II
	AD 256	IMP III
		DACICUS
COS IIII	AD 257	COS III

POSTUMUS	
IMP	AD 258
CAES	
AUG	
P M	
P P	
COS	AD 259

POSTUMUS		GALLIENUS
COS II	AD 260	
COS III	AD 261	COS IIII
		IMP X
	AD 262	COS V
	AD 264	COS VI
	AD 266	COS VII
COS IIII	AD 267	
COS V	AD 268	

CLAUDIUS II:	AURELIAN:
TETRICUS:	TACITUS:
MARIUS:	FLORIANUS:
QUINTILLUS	PROBUS

IMP: CAES: AUG: P M: ...AD 268
P P (Claudius)
COS: IMP: CAES: AUG:
P M: P P (Tetricus) ....AD 268

CLAUDIUS II:
TETRICUS:
MARIUS:
QUINTILLUS

AURELIAN:
TACITUS:
FLORIANUS:
PROBUS

IMP: CAES: AUG:
(Marius)..............................AD 268
IMP: CAES: AUG:
(Quintillus).......................AD 269
          AD 270 (?)......IMP: CAES: AUG:
                              (Aurelian)
          AD 271...........COS (Aurelian)
          AD 274...........COS II (Aurelian)
          AD 275...........COS III (Aurelian)
          AD 275...........IMP: CAES: AUG:
                              P M: COS DES II:
                              P P (Tacitus)
          AD 276...........COS II (Tacitus)
          AD 276...........IMP: CAES: AUG
                              (Florianus)
          AD 276...........IMP: CAES: AUG:
                              P P: P M (Probus)
          AD 277...........COS (Probus)
          AD 278...........COS II (Probus)
          AD 279............COS III (Probus)
          AD 281...........COS IIII (Probus)
          AD 282...........COS V (Probus)

CARUS:
CARINUS:
NUMERIAN:
DIOCLETIAN

MAXIMIAN:
CONSTANTIUS:
GALERIUS

IMP: CAES: AUG: P M: ....AD 282
P P (Carus)
CAES (Carinus)..................AD 282
CAES (Numerian) ....AD 282
COS II (Carus)...................AD 283
AUG: COS: IMP: P M:
P P (Carinus) ....AD 283
AUG: IMP: COS: PP:
(Numerian) ....AD 283
COS II (Carinus)...............AD 284
COS II (Numerian) ....AD 284
IMP: CAES: COS: AUG:
P M: P P (Diocletian) ....AD 284

CARUS: CARINUS: NUMERIAN: DIOCLETIAN		MAXIMIAN: CONSTANTIUS: GALERIUS
COS III (Carinus)	AD 285	
COS II (Diocletian)	AD 285	CAES (Maximianus)
	AD 286	AUG: P M: P P: IMP: CAES: (Maximianus)
COS III (Diocletian)	AD 287	COS (Maximianus)
	AD 288	COS II (Maximianus)
COS IIII (Diocletian)	AD 290	COS III (Maximianus)
	AD 292	COS: CAES (Constantius)
	AD 292	COS: CAES: (Galerius)
COS V (Diocletian)	AD 293	COS IIII (Maximianus)
IMP X (Diocletian)	AD 294	IMP VIIII (Maximianus)
COS VI (Diocletian)	AD 296	COS II (Constantius)
	AD 297	COS V (Maximianus)
	AD 297	COS II (Galerius)
COS VII (Diocletian)	AD 299	COS VI (Maximianus)
	AD 300	COS III (Constantius)
	AD 300	COS III (Galerius)
IMP XVIII (Diocletian)	AD 301	IMP VII (Maximianus)
	AD 302	COS IIII (Constantius)
	AD 302	COS IIII (Galerius)
COS VIII (Diocletian)	AD 303	COS VII (Maximianus)
COS VIIII (Diocletian)	AD 304	COS VIII (Maximianus)
	AD 305	COS V (Constantius)
	AD 305	COS V (Galerius)
	AD 305	IMP: AUG: P M: P P (Constantius and Galerius)

Dates of the Tribunicia Potestas
(Tribunician Power) of the Emperors

(TR P)

AUGUSTUS

TR P, June 27, 23 BC. TR P II, same day and month, 22 BC, and renewed annually on the same date. Thus, at his death in AD 14 he was in the course of his TR P XXXVII.

TIBERIUS

TR P, June 27, 6 BC. Renewed annually until TR P V in 2 BC, TR P VI not until June 27 AD 4. In order to find the year Anno Domini, deduct 2 from the TR P (thus, TR P XXX would be in the year AD 28, or really, AD 28-29 because it was renewed in June of each year and ran to June of the next year).

CALIGULA

TR P, March 18, AD 37. Renewed annually on the same date in the years 38, 39 and 40.

CLAUDIUS I

TR P, January 25, AD 41. Renewed annually on that date. At his death in AD 54, he was in the course of his TR P XIIII.

NERO

TR P, October 13, AD 54. Renewed annually on that date until AD 59, when he apparently started a new system by shortening his TR P VI and counting, thereafter, from December 4 (or 10th?), when he took TR P VII and renewed annually on that date. At his death in June, AD 68, he was in the course of TR P XIIII.

GALBA

TR P only.

OTHO

TR P, only.

VITELLIUS

TR P, only.

VESPASIAN

TR P, July 1, AD 69. Renewed annually on the same date. At his death in June, AD 79, he was in the course of his TR P X.

TITUS

TR P, July 1, AD 71. Renewed annually on the same date. At his death in September, AD 81, he was in the course of his TR P XII.

DOMITIAN
TR P, September 13, AD 81. Renewed annually on the same date. At his death in September, AD 96, he was in the course of his TR P XVI.

NERVA
TR P, September 18, AD 96. TR P II from the same date in the year AD 97. Apparently started TR P III in December of the same year (AD 97). However, some inscriptions, particularly those which are found upon monuments, fail to recognize a TR P III and carry the TR P II to his death on January 25, AD 98.

TRAJAN
TR P, October 27, AD 97. TR P II from December 10, AD 97. Renewed annually on the latter date. At his death in August, AD 117, he was in the course of his TR P XXI.

HADRIAN
TR P from the death of Trajan in August, AD 117. TR P II from December 10, AD 117. Renewed annually on the latter date. At his death on July 10, AD 138, he was in the course of his TR P XXII.

ANTONINUS PIUS
TR P, February 25, AD 138. TR P II, December 10, AD 138, and renewed annually on the latter date. At his death in March, AD 161, he was in the course of his TR P XXIIII.

MARCUS AURELIUS
TR P, February 25, AD 147. TR P II, December 10, AD 147. Renewed annually on the latter date. At his death in March, AD 180, he was in the course of his TR P XXXIIII.

LUCIUS VERUS
TR P, March 7, AD 161. TR P II, December 10, AD 161, and renewed annually on the latter date. At his death in the winter of AD 169 he was in the course of his TR P VIIII.

COMMODUS
TR P, November 27, AD 176. TR P II, December 10, AD 176, and renewed annually on the latter date. At his death in December, AD 192, he was in the course of his TR P XVIII.

PERTINAX
TR P, only.

DIDIUS JULIANUS
TR P, only.

SEPTIMIUS SEVERUS
TR P, June 1, AD 193. TR P II, December 10, AD 193. Renewed annually on the latter date. At his death in February, AD 211, he was in the course of his TR P XVIIII.

CARACALLA
TR P, June 2, AD 198. TR P II, December 10, AD 198, and renewed annually on the latter date. At his death in April (or March?), AD 217, he was in the course of TR P XX.

GETA
TR P, sometime in AD 209. TR P II, December 10, AD 209, renewed annually on the latter date. At his death in April, AD 212, he was in the course of his TR P IIII.

MACRINUS
TR P, April 11, AD 217 to January, 218(?). TR P II from latter date to June 8, AD 218, which was the date of his death.

ELAGABALUS
TR P, AD 218. Renewed annually until his death in AD 222 when he was in the course of TR P V.

SEVERUS ALEXANDER
TR P, March 11, AD 222. Renewed annually, apparently in January of each year. At his death in AD 235 he was in the course of TR P XIIII.

MAXIMINUS
TR P, AD 235. TR P II, AD 236. TR P III, AD 237 (January 16?), TR P IIII, AD 238 (January 16?).

GORDIAN I
TR P, only.

GORDIAN II
TR P, only.

BALBINUS
TR P, only.

PUPIENUS
TR P, only.

GORDIAN III (PIUS)
TR P, AD 238. Renewed annually. At his death in AD 244, he was in the course of TR P VII.

PHILIP I
TR P, March, AD 244. TR P II, January, AD 245. Renewed annually until his death in September or October, AD 249.

TRAJAN DECIUS
Apparently two methods employed here. Either:
1. When saluted emperor by the troops in 248, or
2. From the death of Philip in September or October, 249. He died in 251.

HERENNIUS ETRUSCUS
TR P in 250. Died, November, 251.

HOSTILIAN
TR P in 250. Died, December, 251.

TREBONIANUS GALLUS
Uncertain TR P. Probably November or December, 251. TR P II, 252. TR P IIII (not III), in 253.

VOLUSIAN
Same as his father, Trebonianus Gallus.

VALERIAN AND GALLIENUS
TR P dates are the same for both (father and son). TR P, 253. TR P II, 254. TR P III, 255. Valerian was in the course of TR P VII at his death in 259. Gallienus was in the course of TR P XVI at his death in 268.

POSTUMUS
TR P, 258. TR P II, 259. Renewed annually until his death in 267, when he was in the course of TR P X.

CLAUDIUS II
TR P, 268. Renewed annually. At his death in 270 he was in the course of TR P III.

TETRICUS I
TR P, 270. Renewed annually. At his abdication in 273 he was in the course of TR P III.

AURELIAN
TR P, 270. Renewed annually. At his death in 275 he was in the course of TR P VI.

TACITUS
TR P, September 25, 275. TR P II, January 1, 276.

PROBUS
TR P, probably in 276. Renewed annually. At his death in 282 he was in the course of TR P VII.

CARUS
TR P, 282. TRP II, 283.

CARINUS
TR P, 282. Renewed annually. At his death in 285 he was in the course of TR P III.

NUMERIAN
TR P, 283, TR P II, 284.

DIOCLETIAN
TR P, September 17, 284. TR P II, March 1(?), 285, and renewed annually on the latter date. At his abdication in March, 305, he was in the course of TR P XXII.

MAXIMIAN
Counted his TR P from 285, so that he was always one behind Diocletian (above).

NOTE: The Tribunician power was not assumed by Constantius or Galerius.

BIBLIOGRAPHY OF
ANCIENT GREEK AND ROMAN COINS

SUGGESTED BASIC READING
Sear, David R. *Greek Coins and Their Values,* 2 volumes, 1977-9.
Sear, David R. *Roman Coins and Their Values,* 3rd edition, 1988.

GENERAL INTRODUCTORY REFERENCES
Jenkins, G.K. *Ancient Greek Coins,* revised edition, 1990.
Jones, J.M. *A Dictionary of Ancient Greek Coins,* 1986.
Jones, J.M. *A Dictionary of Ancient Roman Coins.*
Van Meter, David. *Handbook of Roman Imperial Coins,* 1991.
Planat, R.J. *Greek Coin Types and Their Identification,* 1979.
Sear, David R. *Greek Imperial Coins and Their Values,* 1982.
Foss, Clive. *Roman Historical Coins,* 1990.
Burnett, Andrew. *Coinage in the Roman World,* 1987.
Carradice, Ian and Martin Price. *Coinage in the Greek World,* 1988.
Kroh, Dennis J. *Ancient Coin Reference Reviews,* 1993.
Seltman, Charles. *Greek Coins,* 1960.
Mattingly, H. *Roman Coins,* 1928.
Sutherland, C.H. V. *Roman Coins,* 1974.

IMPORTANT STANDARD WORKS
Kraay, Colin. *Archaic and Classical Greek Coins,* 1976.
Morkholm, Otto. *Early Helenistic Coinage,* 1991.
Mattingly, H., Sydenham, E.A. *Roman Imperial Coinage,* 9 volumes, 1923-84.
Crawford, M.H. *Roman Republican Coinage,* 2 volumes, 1974.
Seaby, H.A. and C. King. *Roman Silver Coins,* 5 volumes.
Head, B.V. *Historia Numorum,* 1911.

INDEX A — GREEK

INDEX B — Roman